MEIR WEISS

THE STORY OF JOB'S BEGINNING

Publications of the Perry Foundation for Biblical Research
in the Hebrew University of Jerusalem

The Story

of

Job's Beginning

Job 1-2: A Literary Analysis

by

Meir Weiss

JERUSALEM 1983
THE MAGNES PRESS, THE HEBREW UNIVERSITY

©

By The Magnes Press
The Hebrew University

Jerusalem 1983

ISBN 965-223-438-9
Printed in Israel
at Astronel Press, Jerusalem

To the memory of Rafi

CONTENTS

Preface to the English Translation

The Hebrew version of *The Story of Job's Beginning* appeared in Jerusalem in 1969 as Booklet No. 40 of a series entitled *Iyyunim Lamadrich Velamoreh*, published under the auspices of the Youth Aliyah Department of the Jewish Agency. The English translation was undertaken by the Research Committee of the Faculty of Humanities at the Hebrew University of Jerusalem in December 1974, just two months after the death of my son Raphael (Rafi).

Though I originally dedicated this work to the memory of my students who perished in the Holocaust, the publication of *The Story of Job's Beginning* in its English version is an apt occasion for me to extend the dedication to the memory of the student from whom I learned most of all, my late son. Not only was the book written at his insistence, but it was also he who proposed the original title, *Hasippur al Reshito shel Iyyov*, from the statement that "the LORD blessed Job's latter end more than his beginning" (Job 42:12). Though Rafi, too, was saved from "the valley of the shadow of death" and walked "in the land of the living" — in both the literal sense (see Psalm 116:9) and the midrashic, that is, in the Land of Israel (see *Yalqut Shimoni, ad loc.*) and in Jerusalem, yet — he was cut off from "the land of the living" at the age of thirty-four, succumbing finally to the illness which had been his lot since childhood, a consequence of the horrors of deportation and the ghetto.

The present study is based on my lectures entitled "Selected Chapters in the Book of Job", delivered at the Hebrew University of Jerusalem in 1966-67. Because of the popular nature of the series for which this study was originally composed in its Hebrew version, I have for the most part

9

omitted citing the sources of the suggestions and interpretations, both traditional and modern, which appear throughout the commentaries. I have likewise refrained from expressing any explicit agreement or disagreement with existing opinion, and have not included debate on linguistic points, except in such cases as seemed desirable for contextual or didactic reasons. Additional references and commentary would be unnecessary since, like the Hebrew original, the English translation is designed primarily for the use of teachers and students. The teacher will find it useful to consult complementary exegesis and for this purpose I have appended a list of suggested commentaries and a select bibliography, p. 83.

The English translation of the biblical text is essentially that found in *The Book of Job, A New Translation*, Philadelphia, The Jewish Publication Society of America, 1980. The deviations that occur are necessitated by exegetical considerations.

The poet Solomon Ibn Gabirol wrote: "My heart desired to thank You — but was unable". I can but echo these words as I attempt to convey my gratitude to all who have been connected with the English translation of *The Story of Job's Beginning*.

First and foremost, I thank all the members of the Research Committee of the Faculty of Humanities at the Hebrew University, without whose support this work could not have been undertaken. I am particularly indebted to the late Professor Haim Hillel Ben-Sasson ז״ל who, as head of the Institute of Jewish Studies, prompted the original decision to translate the work into English. I am likewise grateful to Professor Jacob Sussman, who graciously saw to it that the task was fully accomplished.

Mrs. Ruth Rigbi and her daughter Miss Elisheva Rigbi toiled devotedly at the labor of translation. The final form of the English version is essentially the product of the skill, wisdom, and dedication of Mr. Baruch Schwartz. Mr. J. Frank generously applied his erudition to the task of stylizing the text, ensuring that the English version preserved the flavor of the original, and Mr. S. Reem provided most helpful suggestions concerning matters of typography. I am indebted to them all and thankfully acknowledge their painstaking efforts.

It is a pleasure to make note of the generous support offered by the Perry Foundation to the publication of this work. Last but not least, I

owe a very great debt of gratitude to Professor Haim Beinart, chairman
of the Magnes Press, and to its director, Mr. Ben Zion Yehoshua, for including *The Story of Job's Beginning* among the Magnes publications.

צדקתם תעמוד לעד — להגדיל תורה ולהאדירה.

Jerusalem,
Eighth anniversary of the death of Rafi Weiss
(10 Marḥeshvan 5743)

11

From the Preface to the Hebrew Edition

This study presents an analysis of the prose prologue to the book of Job. Critical analyses of this story have more than once attempted to reveal its ancient form, to discover the time and place of its creation, to distinguish between earlier and later components and between intentional and inadvertent interpolations. Attempts have also been made to determine the antecedent literary form employed by the author to give shape to his ideas. In this way scholars have tried to learn about the history of the narrative, the manner of its creation and even the intentions of its author and redactors. Critics have scrutinized the story from an aesthetic perspective in an endeavor to abstract its fundamental formal aspects, to classify, categorize and analyze them, to evaluate the stylistic embellishments and literary style and the beauty and majesty of the story, so as to assess the artistic skill of the author and the aesthetic merit of his work.

My analysis is not concerned with the story's *becoming* but with its *being*, not with the development *of* the work but rather with the development of ideas and emotions *within* it. It is not the components themselves which engage me, but their arrangement, and my analysis of the story's form is not intended to strip form from content but rather to show its immanence in the story: how form and content interrelate and interact, that is, how the character and the organizing principle of the story derive from its form, and how form determines the arrangement of the basic elements within the whole and their relationship to the whole, and moulds whatever is expressed therein.

I do not intend to assess the story from without, from either an historic or an aesthetic point of view, but rather from within, from the story itself. Thus I will not present an historical explanation for any metamorphoses

13

it has undergone, nor will I offer an aesthetic evaluation. My concern is to understand its meaning — not necessarily the intention of the writer but the intention of the *story*, as expressed through its words and its structure, that is, by its external architecture and internal tectonics.

The story serves as prologue to the book of Job; in it are formulated the assumptions upon which the entire book is based and according to which everything that follows is to be understood. Opinion differs as to the relationship between the prologue and the body of the book; while my analysis will treat the prologue as an independent entity, my assumption is that upon this very analysis rests our ability to determine whether the connection between the two parts of the book is in fact organic.

In reverence and awe, I dedicate this book to the sacred memory of those of my own students and congregants who were among the six million of our brothers and sisters, sons and daughters, martyred when Satan's whirlwind came from the wilderness that was the West and struck the four corners of the house of Judah, toppling it upon its inhabitants. I offer this work to our teachers, in appreciation of the sacred service they perform.

May our people, the Job of nations, likewise be blessed more at its latter end than it was at its beginning.

Jerusalem,
Holocaust Remembrance Day, 5727

THE STORY OF JOB'S BEGINNING
(Job 1-2)

Even a casual look at the first two chapters of Job reveals that they are a literary unit, comprising five sections that resemble the scenes of a play. And since these two chapters serve as prologue to the book, the five scenes may be viewed as the first act of a play. Although brief and sparsely sketched, the five scenes succeed in establishing the dramatic situation from which all that is contained in the book develops and proceeds:

Scene I	1:1-5	Job's way of life and his fortune
Scene II	1:6-12	The first dialogue between God and Satan about Job
Scene III	1:13-22	Job in the first phase of his trial
Scene IV	2:1-11	The second dialogue between God and Satan about Job
Scene V	2:12-13 [3:1]	Job in the second phase of his trial

The setting alternates between heaven and earth with more scenes taking place on earth: the opening and closing scenes take place on earth. This alone suggests that the aim of the story is to portray events here on earth rather than those on high. Heavenly events serve only to reflect and elucidate earthly ones, alternating with and responding to them.

While the three earthly scenes portray Job in his prosperity and in his adversity, the two heavenly scenes serve to reveal to the reader what is hidden from the players, namely, the transcendent backdrop to events on earth; this in itself is indicative of the problem with which the book grapples. For· although God is the protagonist in heaven and Job the protagonist on earth, both God and Job are present in all five scenes; even

15

where they do not appear or speak, their presence is felt through mention and reference. It is with the relationship between these two protagonists, God and Job, that the prologue is concerned, as is the entire book.

While God is certainly predominant in Job's speech, thought and action, for God, Job is a single and exclusive preoccupation, which indicates that Job is in fact the focus of the prologue and that he alone is the hero of the story.

Scene I
(1:1-5)

This section presents Job's way of life and his fortune. Verses 1-2 are biographical, giving information on Job's name, home, and family status. But they also raise two questions: how does the narrator come to know these facts, and why does he mention them? As to the first, scholars agree that the narrator did not invent Job. He was familiar with both the name and the character, either as an historic personage or as a legendary figure from written or oral tradition, which he used in part as raw material for his story. One of Ezekiel's prophecies (14:14, 20) lends support to the accepted view that in biblical times, at least at certain periods and in certain circles, various legends which portrayed Job as the prototype of the perfectly upright man were widespread.[1] Indeed, the opening verse of the

---

1. Had Ezekiel's listeners known the fate of Job as our story – or its ancient source – tells it, the prophet could not have mentioned Job at all. Placing him alongside Daniel and Noah, Ezekiel clearly intends to illustrate the doctrine of individual reward and punishment and to dispel the people's illusion that the merit of the fathers will save the children from retribution. "Though Noah, Daniel and Job were in it, as I live, says the LORD God, they shall save neither son nor daughter; they shall save their own selves alone by their righteousness" (Ezekiel 14:20). In our tale, Job's children do not sin, they are righteous, yet they do not save themselves. Moreover, the story tells us, Job, though spared death, suffers serious affliction. Our Job, therefore, could not have served as proof of the doctrine that Ezekiel, in referring to him, wished to propagate, i.e. that a man's lot is determined by his deeds alone. Nor can we assume that the circumstances of our story derive from Ezekiel's prophecy or from the same legend from which the prophet drew: a Job saved by his virtue could hardly have served our narrator's purpose. There probably circulated many legends about the righteous Job which told of the hero's lot in many and varied ways.

story, as an examination of its structure will show, reinforces the assumption that the original readers of the book were already acquainted with the person of Job, whose righteousness had won him such renown. As for the second question, it would appear that the author's purpose in mentioning Job's name and abode is essentially informative — the "flight from anonymity",[2] which is frequently found in folk legends, especially with reference to the main character.

But the commentator has also to consider whether such biographical details, in addition to their strictly formal function, serve another, thematic purpose, which contributes more significantly to a proper understanding of the story. The peculiar structure of verse 1a proves that they do.

A man there was in the land of Uz;	אִישׁ הָיָה בְאֶרֶץ עוּץ
Job was his name.	אִיּוֹב שְׁמוֹ

(1:1a)

A comparison with the opening sentence of I Samuel demonstrates the uniqueness of our verse:

There was a man from Ramathaim-	וַיְהִי אִישׁ אֶחָד מִן־הָרָמָתַיִם צוֹפִים
Zophim in the hill-country of Ephraim	מֵהַר אֶפְרָיִם
and his name was Elkana...	וּשְׁמוֹ אֶלְקָנָה

(I Samuel 1:1)

The book of Job, to quote David Yellin, "begins with a measured verse consisting of three short, two-word members, each containing three syllables and penultimate stress, with the emphasis upon the word of greatest importance: אִישׁ הָיָה 'A man there was.' The style thus becomes light and vivid.... The alternative ויהי איש בארץ עוץ ושמו איוב 'There was a man in the Land of Uz and his name was Job' would have detracted much from the movement and brevity".[3]

These remarks on the style of the opening verse are correct as far as they go, dealing essentially with the aesthetic aspect of the style. But there is more to style than this. Style is also expressive. Not only the artistic value of the verse has to be determined, but also the meaning it conveys;

2. See Y. Heinemann, דרכי האגדה[2], Jerusalem 1954, p. 20.
3. חקרי מקרא, I: *Job*, Jerusalem 1927, p. 1.

it is not enough merely to note that, were the opening verse of Job parallel to that of I Samuel, it would lose "movement and brevity". We should also ask: Apart from the actual information conveyed, what is implied in "A man there was ... Job was his name" which is not implied in "There was a man ... and his name was Elkana"?

To determine the meaning inherent in the peculiar structure of Job 1:1 in contrast to that of I Samuel 1:1, we shall turn first to Esther 2:5, which is similar to our verse:

A Jew there was in Shushan the fortress	אִישׁ יְהוּדִי הָיָה בְּשׁוּשַׁן הַבִּירָה
and his name was Mordecai	וּשְׁמוֹ מָרְדְּכַי

The sentence indeed bears a likeness to our verse, though it is not identical. What is expressed in Job in two sentences is expressed in Esther in one. In Job — איוב שמו "Job was his name": an independent clause, predicate and subject; in Esther — ושמו מרדכי "and his name was Mordecai", part of a compound sentence, subject and predicate (as in I Samuel 1:1 ושמו אלקנה "and his name was Elkana"). Thus the verse in Esther begins like the one in Job, differently from that in I Samuel, and it ends like the verse in I Samuel, differently from that in Job. As we have seen, the identical beginnings in Job and Esther can be explained on metric grounds (Yellin: the purpose is "to put the stress on the main point"). But can the different endings of the two verses be likewise accounted for, on aesthetic grounds alone? Evidence to the contrary can be seen in the occurrence of many clauses which are informationally and structurally identical to the one in Job, for example:

A champion of the Philistine forces stepped forward;	וַיֵּצֵא אִישׁ־הַבֵּנַיִם מִמַּחֲנוֹת פְּלִשְׁתִּים
Goliath was his name, of Gath	גָּלְיָת שְׁמוֹ מִגַּת

(I Samuel 17:4)

The text does not read "And his name was Goliath of Gath" [ושמו גלית מגת]. Similarly "Nabal was his name [שמו נבל]" (I Samuel 25:25); "A man from the hill-country of Ephraim, Sheba the son of Bichri is his name" [איש מהר אפרים שבע בן בכרי שמו] (II Samuel 20:21); "A son is to be born to the House of David, Josiah [will be] his name" [הנה בן נולד לבית דוד יאשיהו שמו] (I Kings 13:2); and finally, a sentence

18

which recurs several times in the Bible, שמו ה' "The LORD is His name" (Exodus 15:3; Jeremiah 33:2; Amos 5:8, 9:6). Identical structure expresses identical meaning. What, then, is the implicit meaning of a sentence which, in naming someone, makes the name, the predicate, precede the subject, שמו "his name"?

The answer must be prefaced by a syntactical note. In clauses such as these, known as nominal clauses, the standard order is subject-predicate, e.g. "The LORD is our king" [ה' מלכנו] (Isaiah 33:22); "the season is rainy" [והעת גשמים] (Ezra 10:13); "I am a few men" [ואני מתי מספר] (Genesis 34:30); "your heart is not with me" [ולבך אין אתי] (Judges 16:15); "his name was Elkana" [ושמו אלקנה] (I Samuel 1:1); "his name was Mordecai" [ושמו מרדכי] (Esther 2:5); etc. In our verse, however, "Job was his name" [איוב שמו], as in other similar verses – "the LORD is his name", "Goliath was his name", "Zemach will be his name" (Zachariah 6:12) — and nominal clauses of other types, e.g. "for *dust* you are" [כי עפר אתה] (Genesis 3:19); "my *sister* are you" [אחותי את] (Genesis 12:13); "truly my bone and flesh are you" [אך עצמי ובשרי אתה] (Genesis 29:14), etc., the regular order of nominal clauses is reversed. Why? It is immediately apparent that the effect of the inversion is to emphasize the predicate: אחותי את — "you are my *sister*" (not my wife); כי עפר אתה — "you are *dust*" (nothing more); עצמי ובשרי אתה — "you are *my bone and flesh*" (not a stranger).

The anomalous placing of the proper name before the subject in "Job was his name", "Zemach will be his name" etc., indicates a deliberate effort to highlight the name. It is the emotional impact alone which distinguishes sentences like "and his name was Elkana" and "and his name was Mordecai" from "the LORD is His name" and "Job was his name". The first type simply imparts information concerning the man in question; the second type is intended not merely — if, indeed, at all — to impart information, but rather to convey something more, or something other, than that which would have been expressed had the name appeared in its usual position. By saying of her husband, "Nabal is his name", Abigail is certainly not trying to tell David her husband's name — David already knows it — but rather to draw to David's attention the meaning of the name Nabal, "churlishness", for she goes on to say: ונבלה עמו — "churlishness is with him". Such emphasis on a word is an indication that what is being conveyed is its full and precise significance, especially when the word is a proper name whose original, root meaning has been forgotten or at least neglected in conventional, everyday speech.

Such is evidently the case with ה׳ שמו ("the LORD is His name"). It can hardly be presumed that the sentence is intended to inform us of God's name. This would be meaningless in context: what could be the point of such a sentence as "The LORD is a man of war, the LORD is His name" (Exodus 15:3)? Our assumption, namely, that emphasizing the name by placing it at the beginning of the sentence serves to call attention to its etymology, rests on structural evidence (ה׳ שמו and not ושמו ה׳) as well as contextual evidence. The Tetragrammaton is stressed so that its root meaning — היה "to be" as explained in Exodus 3:14 — may be understood; that is, to say of God "as His name is, so He is" (cf. Abigail's words about Nabal, above): *Being*, here, being with us (Rosenzweig-Buber).

As for the hero's name, איוב or Job, it has often been suggested (even in critical scholarship) that it is symbolic, being a passive form of the verb איב "to hate", and its meaning is "one who is hated", "one who has enemies" (just as from the verb ילד "to bear", the noun יִלֹד means "one who is born", "a child").[4] Indeed, Job's words ותחשבני לאויב לך "You consider me Your enemy" (13:24) do contain a play on words איוב (Job)/אויב ("enemy"), as shown by the Midrash: "Said Job to God: Master of the Universe! Have You confused Iyyob (איוב, Job) with Oyeb (enemy)?" (*Talmud Bab., Baba Batra* 16a). But Job is not Heaven's enemy, nor does he make Heaven his enemy, neither in our story nor in the rest of the book, and it is unlikely that the author, if he chose a symbolic name for his hero, would have chosen one that contradicts the story. We should rather expect him to choose one that reflects the hero's character, or his fate, or the lesson to be learned from his life.

But accenting the etymological root of the name is only one of the possible roles of sentences of the type איוב שמו. Another possibility re-

---

4. The first to interpret the name Job in this manner was R. Zerachya of Barcelona (late 13th century) in his commentary on Job (published by I. Schwarz in תקות אנוש, Berlin 1898, p. 169, a collection of commentaries on Job). Most recently this same interpretation has been supported by N. H. Tur-Sinai (ספּוּ איוב, Tel Aviv 1954; also "איוב" in: אנציקלופדיה מקראית, I, Jerusalem 1950, p. 244).

mains: that, as in our case, the stress on the name indicates a *certain person*, one of many bearing that name, a person with whom the reader is particularly acquainted. Such is the case in the sentence הנה בן נולד לבית דוד יאשיהו שמו "a son is to be born to the House of David, Josiah his name" (I Kings 13:2). Here the phrase יאשיהו שמו "Josiah [will be] his name" sounds completely different from the alternative ושמו יאשיהו "and his name [will be] Josiah". It does not merely offer information as to the name of the scion to be born, any more than the sentence ה' שמו "the LORD is His name" offers information as to the name of God. But neither does it – unlike the phrase ה' שמו "the LORD is His name" – emphasize the etymology of the name. Whoever made the statement יאשיהו שמו "Josiah will be his name" was referring to *the* Josiah told of in II Kings 23. By emphasizing the name, he indicates that this scion, whose birth to the house of David is foretold, is the very same Josiah who is to gain renown by destroying the high places. Similarly, when Joab tells the wise woman "A man from the hill-country of Ephraim, Sheba the son of Bichri is his name, has rebelled against King David", he obviously does not intend to inform the woman of the rebel's name, which everyone already knew, but to say that it is this particular and well-known individual who is wanted. The same holds for Goliath in the sentence גלית שמו "Goliath is his name" (I Samuel 17:4), which means Goliath, the infamous, the well-known.

Now, if we recall that Job, too, was a common name, as evidenced by its appearance in a pre-Hebrew form in ancient Near Eastern archeological finds (Middle Bronze Age), it is logical to conclude that the author, wishing to refer to this particular Job, famous in some connection, used the introductory formula איוב שמו "Job was his name" instead of ושמו איוב "and his name was Job", so as to draw the reader's attention to this one among the many bearers of the name Job. Moreover, bearing in mind that legends about Job the righteous were current prior to our story, we may conclude that the order of the words in the opening verse serves to single out this specific, famous, righteous Job.

בְּאֶרֶץ עוּץ "In the land of Uz": While we may conclude from the structure of the opening sentence that the name of the protagonist is borrowed from another source, we shall see that the name of his country is imaginary and original to this story. It is commonly accepted that the portrayal of Job as a non-Jew is explained by his prominent role in the ancient legend.[5] In the prophecy of Ezekiel (Chapter 14), Job is likewise depicted as a non-Jew to be compared with Noah and Daniel, alongside whom he is mentioned. The fact that the narrator assigned to Job a dwelling-place in a foreign land can be explained as a "flight from anonymity" (see above, p. 17), but the choice of the Land of Uz demands explanation, as does the fact that this is not a city but a country.

There are a number of traditions as to the location of Job's place of residence, but they all relate to two principal regions: either Hauran, to the northeast, in the territory of Aram, east of the Jordan river, or else in the south, on the borders of Edom and Arabia. In the Bible there is no conclusive evidence as to the exact geographical location of "the Land of Uz"; apart from our verse, "the Land of Uz" appears only in poetry – Lamentations 4:21 and Jeremiah 25:20, and in both cases the ancient Versions do not refer to "the Land of Uz". In Lamentations, Uz is the dwelling-place of Edom; in Jeremiah, it is mentioned before Philistia and

---

5. According to A. Cahana in his commentary on Job (pp. 22-23), and M. H. Segal (מבוא המקרא, Jerusalem 1964, p. 635), the reason for portraying Job as a Gentile is apologetic, namely, that one who ponders the attributes of God and questions His righteousness could not possibly be a Jew. But this explanation is clearly untenable. For the conceptual structure of the story is based on the perception of Job as "blameless and upright, one who fears God and shuns evil"; it is further said of him "there is no one like him on earth". He is the ideal religious figure. The stability of the structure would be undermined were the architect to perceive Job's doubts as even the slightest flaw in the perfection of his faith and therefore to portray him as a non-Jew, going out of his way to do so. To portray a non-Jew as the prototype of one who fears God and fears sin would seem to imply an explanation opposite to that given by Segal and Cahana. The protagonist of the story is represented as a Gentile and not a Jew in order to teach that perfect fear of heaven is not solely the possession of the Jews. God calls Job "My servant" like whom there is no one on earth, even though he belongs to another people. And indeed, to illustrate this universal viewpoint on the religious appraisal of man, Job is mentioned alongside Noah and Daniel in the prophecy of Ezekiel. These three men, who are not Jews, and not three others, who are, are presented by the prophet as examples of righteous men, in order that we might realize that in the eyes of God, affiliation with the Jewish people is not the deciding factor. This universalistic idea is clear in the prophecy of Ezekiel. But the concern of the story of Job is to show the reaction of the perfectly righteous man to the occurrences which affront the belief in divine justice, and not to teach the universality of the fear of God. Therefore it would appear that this is not the intention of the narrator in portraying his protagonist as a non-Jew.

22

Edom, but in this instance its authenticity is doubtful. Uz also appears as a personal name in genealogical records; here, too, are reflected the two traditional possibilities: Uz is a descendant of Seir (in Edom, see Genesis 36:21, 28; II Chronicles 1:42) or Aram (Genesis 10:23; 22:21; I Chronicles 1:17). In any case, the "Land of Uz" is located east of the Jordan River, as implied by the statement that Job was "greater than all the people of the East" (1:3). The "people of the East" mentioned here were the desert tribes who lived in the Syrian desert, east of Ammon, Moab and Seir, in an area extending north to Mesopotamia and south beyond Arabia Petraea and Arabia Felix.

Why, then, did the narrator choose the Land of Uz? And furthermore, if the Land of Uz is Edom, why did he not call the place by its politically acceptable, geographical, "official" appellation — Edom — or by its synonym — Seir? Or if the Land of Uz is Aram, why did he not call it Aram? And why did he place Job not in a specific city, but in Uz, a land apparently called by its poetic name?

Evidently, the narrator chose the *Land* of Uz, that is, a country and not a city, and specifically Uz and not any other land, because this name best suited his purpose. The name must have evoked the associations most appropriate to the narrator's intention. In order to discover the meaning implicit in the name "the Land of Uz" one must attempt to uncover the associative capacity of the name Uz. One of the primary factors of association — especially in the Bible — is the aural effect, and the etymology based on it. Thus we must first explore the possibility that the principal association in the use of ארץ עוץ "the Land of Uz" in our story is contained in the *sound* of the word עוץ "Uz", in particular, in a popular etymology based on its similarity to the word עֵצָה "council", "wisdom". The term עֵצָה, a leading concept in the Wisdom literature of the Bible, has several times prompted the suggestion that "the Land of Uz" as it appears here is to be interpreted in this connection.[6] This may be shown to be the correct, or at least the probable, meaning of the name of Job's homeland if it is corroborated not only by the context in which it appears, but by the story in its totality — in other words, by every detail of content and style.

6. Rashi; Maimonides, *Guide to the Perplexed* III:2; R. Zerachya of Barcelona. See J. Derenbourg in *Revue des Études Juives*, I (1880), p. 3.

And indeed, more than one detail in the story lends credence to the above theory; viewed from this perspective, several details that are formally organic but thematically superfluous, including the mention of "the Land of Uz" itself, take on a significance that is organically consonant with the theme of the story and even complements it. The following examples give a clear illustration:

1. The Land of Uz, according to Lamentations, is the home of Edom. Both the name and genealogy of Eliphaz the Temanite, one of Job's three friends, are associated with Edom (Genesis 36:10, 11, 15; I Chronicles 1:35, 36 and Genesis 36:11, Jeremiah 49:7, 20; Ezekiel 25:13; Amos 1:12; Obadiah 9). Edom and Teman are considered centers of wisdom in the Bible (Jeremiah 49:7; Obadiah 8).

2. Job is described as "greater than all the people of the East" (1:3).That the greatness of "the people of the East" refers to their wisdom can be understood from the verse "Solomon's wisdom exceeded the wisdom of all the people of the East" (I Kings 5:10).

3. The conceptual starting-point of the story (and of the entire book) is the world of Wisdom literature. The story's (and the book's) purpose is to dispute the conventional claims of Wisdom, and specifically that outlook whose basic principle is expressed in the sentence צדיק וטוב לו, the righteous man is blessed with good — material good, first and foremost.

From the above we may conclude with reasonable certainty that the suggestion is correct: the narrator's reason for choosing "the Land of Uz" as the home of Job, and the meaning expressed therein, is that "the Land of Uz" is Edom, the land of "Wisdom", and in the name Uz is echoed Wisdom's concept of עֵצָה, "council". The aim is to establish that Job, the archetype of he who fears Heaven and dreads sin, lived in the world of Wisdom.

The attributes of the story's protagonist, which in verse 1a are merely implied by means of emotional, stylistic devices, receive explicit formulation, both verbally and conceptually, in verse 1b and verses 2-3, further supporting our conclusions as to the meaning of verse 1a. Verse 1b gives a concrete illustration of what was stated or implied in the sentence "Job was his name", while verses 2-3 contain the application of verse 1b according to verse 1a, since according to the teachings current in Uz, such a man as is referred to, both implicitly and explicitly, in verse 1b must have, as his lot in life, what is specified in verses 2-3.

24

| That man was blameless and upright; | וְהָיָה הָאִישׁ הַהוּא תָּם וְיָשָׁר |
| he feared God and shunned evil. | וִירֵא אֱלֹהִים וְסָר מֵרָע |

(1:1b)

Job has four attributes as defined in the two couplets: 1) תם וישר "blameless and upright"; 2) ירא אלהים וסר מרע "fearing God and shunning evil". The first couplet contains one-word expressions; in the second, each expression consists of two words. The four expressions are common terms in the doctrine of the Wisdom school: by defining Job as possessing these four characteristics, the story defines him as having those attributes which are desirable according to the Wisdom ideal. The first two, "blameless and upright", are a general description which is more precisely stated in the second pair. Job was "blameless". Innocence, integrity and not duplicity — this is the primary attribute upon which all the other good qualities depend. תם "blameless" refers to his character; ישר "upright" to his actions. He is upright in that he does not deviate from the straight path, he does not follow crooked ways. These qualities derive from the fear of God and are manifested in the shunning of evil. Fear of God in the Bible — with the exception of the book of Ecclesiastes — is not just dread of God but the feeling of the religious experience (I. Heinemann). He who fears God is constantly aware that there is "an eye that sees and an ear that hears".

| Seven sons and three daughters | וַיִּוָּלְדוּ לוֹ שִׁבְעָה בָנִים וְשָׁלוֹשׁ בָּנוֹת |
| were born to him. | |

(1:2)

Job's righteousness was perfect and complete, hence his reward had to be perfect and complete. And so it was. He was blessed with happiness and wealth: first of all with children, both sons and daughters. His sons were seven, his daughters three — numbers which, as is well known, had symbolic importance among the ancient Near Eastern peoples in general, and in Israel in particular. Seven is considered a round number, a whole (compare I Samuel 2:5; Ruth 4:15); likewise the number three indicates a complete unit. Not only did Job have sons and daughters, but he had a perfect number of them; thus the verse is telling us that Job's blessing was complete. Moreover, the combined number of sons and daughters is also indicative of perfect blessing, since the number ten is also perceived as a perfect number.

Job's material wealth was also complete:

His possessions were seven thousand sheep,	וַיְהִי מִקְנֵהוּ שִׁבְעַת אַלְפֵי־צֹאן
three thousand camels,	וּשְׁלֹשֶׁת אַלְפֵי גְמַלִּים
five hundred yoke of oxen,	וַחֲמֵשׁ מֵאוֹת צֶמֶד־בָּקָר
and five hundred she-asses,	וַחֲמֵשׁ מֵאוֹת אֲתוֹנוֹת
and a very great household	וַעֲבֻדָּה רַבָּה מְאֹד

(1:3a)

The total of each pair of animals is ten (3+7, 5+5), a perfect number, and each type in itself comprises a perfect number. In other words, there was nothing lacking, neither from any of the parts nor from the whole. Furthermore, sheep and camels are usually the property of nomadic tribes, whereas tillers of the land own oxen and asses. From this, too, we may gather that Job's fortune was consummate. In addition, he had עבדה רבה מאד "a very great household", that is, manservants and maidservants, who constituted a great intellectual as well as physical resource. While of Isaac it is related that he had עבדה רבה "a great household" (Genesis 26:14), it is said of Job that he had a עבדה רבה מאד "a *very* great household", and the verse concludes:

so that this man was greater than all the people of the East.	וַיְהִי הָאִישׁ הַהוּא גָּדוֹל מִכָּל־בְּנֵי־קֶדֶם

(1:3b)

According to the Targum and the majority of classical and modern commentators, the meaning of "a very great household" is that Job had abundant property. This is the meaning in the parallel case of Isaac: "The man became great, and grew greater and greater until he became very great" (Genesis 26:13), where the context indicates that Isaac's greatness was in his wealth. Indeed, גדול "great" often denotes affluence, as in the case of Nabal (I Samuel 25:2), of Barzilay (II Samuel 19:33) and of the Shunnamite woman (I Kings 4:8). If this is the case here, then the phrase "so that this man was greater than all the people of the East" resumes what was said earlier. However, it is not this interpretation — given by the overwhelming majority of commentators — which is the correct meaning of the verse, but rather, the less popular interpretation:[7] that the reference is to greatness in *wisdom*. This idea is reinforced by the wording of the sentence itself: a) Greatness is brought into the verse as an independent entity; the syntactical construction of the verse implies that we are dealing with something distinct from what was mentioned in the previous sentence; b) The phrasing of the verse implies that it refers to wisdom: Job is defined by comparison with "the people of the East", and as we have seen, the greatness of the "people of the East" lay in their wisdom (compare I Kings 5:10). It does not say that Job was *wiser* "than all the people of the East" but that he was "*greater*" than them, for the sentence wishes to convey not only that he was wise, but that he was honored and respected by the people of the East, amongst whom it was surely a man of outstanding wisdom that was considered great. Honorable social status is the greatest blessing that a man can attain in this world.

That Job's worldly riches are concomitant with his good qualities is also clear from the number of each. The four good qualities described above correspond to the four pairs of wordly riches: sons and daughters, sheep and camels, oxen and asses, household, and greatness, in both wisdom and status.

The first three verses that introduce the protagonist tell of Job's life and fortune at the time of the story's beginning, but they also hint at the future. Careful examination of the wording reveals that what is to happen is foretold at the outset. Concerning Job's familial bliss, we are told "Seven sons and three daughters were born to him" (verse 2). The full significance of the verse is to be found not in its content but in its wording, as emerges from a comparison between this verse and the wording of another sentence in our book which likewise speaks of Job's joy in his family: "He had also seven sons and three daughters" (42:13). The verse at the beginning of the story relates only that these children were *born* to Job, and not that he *had* them, for the story proceeds to tell of their death. Furthermore, with reference to Job's attributes, the story tells us: "that man was (והיה) blameless and upright" (verse 1), while it is with the words "that man was (ויהי) greater etc." that we learn about Job's material and social situation. Both והיה and ויהי indicate past events.

---

7. Rabbi Yosef Kimchi.

27

Now, according to the conventional use of verb tenses in the Bible, if, at the beginning of the story, the verb which is used as a predicate is in the *qatal* (perfect) form, then the verb that follows will be used in the *vayyiqtol* (converted imperfect) form, as in the example . . . והנחש היה ערום ויאמר אל האשה "Now the serpent was the shrewdest . . . and he said to the woman" (Genesis 3:1); "He was (היה) a mighty hunter . . . and the head of his kingdom was (ותהי) . . . " (Genesis 10:9-10); " . . . the word of the LORD came (היה) to Abram . . . and Abram said (ויאמר)" (Genesis 15:1-2). According to this procedure, the wording here should have been "A man there was (איש היה) in the Land of Uz . . . and the man was (ויהי האיש)" etc.; not, as it stands, והיה האיש. This anomaly has a significance which derives from the precise meaning of the *qatal* (perfect) form of the verb as opposed to the *vayyiqtol* (converted imperfect) form. Although both indicate an action done in the past, the *qatal* form also indicates that the action was not an isolated one, nor an action that repeated itself several times, but rather a permanent condition. The idea conveyed by the unusual use of the verb tenses in the verse on Job's personal characteristics, and by the conventional verb usage in those verses which speak of his wealth and honor, is that his character was consistent while his wealth and honor existed once but were lost, in other words, his material and social status were but temporary. Hence our story's beginning intimates at what will be revealed at its end.

His sons would go to feast,	וְהָלְכוּ בָנָיו וְעָשׂוּ מִשְׁתֶּה
each in his own home on his day;	בֵּית אִישׁ יוֹמוֹ
they would send to invite their three sisters	וְשָׁלְחוּ וְקָרְאוּ לִשְׁלֹשֶׁת אַחְיֹתֵיהֶם
to eat and drink with them.	לֶאֱכֹל וְלִשְׁתּוֹת עִמָּהֶם

(1:4)

What is referred to in general terms in the first two verses is described in concrete terms in verses 4-5. These confirm and complement the earlier portrayal of Job's wealth and happiness. For the image now taking shape shows the reader that this happiness lacked nothing. Not only was Job blessed with sons and daughters, and with the privilege of seeing each of them happily settled in his own home; he was also blessed in seeing brotherly and sisterly affection abiding among them. His children are

always together;[8] Job, however, is absent. Job's happiness can be complete only if his sons' happiness is complete; therefore, when they gather
together, he is not present. Otherwise, his sons would no doubt take his
presence into account, and this consideration might inhibit their natural
joy. Indeed, making a point of Job's absence from the feasts not only
emphasizes his tact, but also indicates his confidence that his children will
do no wrong, neither in word nor in deed. His absence is an important
detail, for not only does it shed light on what is to be related in verse 5,
but it also enables us to understand the events to come and the difficulties
that are to arise.

Verse 4 describes an idyllic situation in Job's family: its function is to
illustrate his happiness. Verse 5 portrays Job's scrupulous fear of sin,
stressing that even in the midst of his greatest joy he was concerned with
serving God: its function is to illustrate his righteousness.

When the cycle of feast-days was complete,	וַיְהִי כִּי הִקִּיפוּ יְמֵי הַמִּשְׁתֶּה
Job sent to them and sanctified them,	וַיִּשְׁלַח אִיּוֹב וַיְקַדְּשֵׁם
and arose early in the morning	וְהִשְׁכִּים בַּבֹּקֶר
and offered burnt offerings,	וְהֶעֱלָה עֹלוֹת
one for each of them;	מִסְפַּר כֻּלָּם

(1:5a)

In the main clause of this complex sentence, the first two predicates
(וישלח "sent" and ויקדשם "sanctified") are verbs in the *vayyiqtol* (converted imperfect) form; the last two (השכים "arose" and והעלה "offered") are
in the *qatal* (perfect) form. This change of forms is not intended "to effect
some variation in style and put more life" into the sentence (Yellin), but
rather to express a change in aspect. The verbs that appear in the *qatal*
form express actions that occurred before those appearing in the *vayyiqtol*
form. Therefore, the meaning of the sentence is: when the period of
feasting had passed, after the feast in the home of the seventh son ended
and before the next round commenced in the home of the first, Job rose up
early in the morning and offered burnt offerings, and afterwards he sent

8. All the verbs are in the *qatal* (perfect); see above on verse 3b.

29

for his sons "and sanctified them", and summoned them. All this for what purpose?

for Job thought,
"Perhaps my sons have sinned,
and ברכו God in their hearts."

כִּי אָמַר אִיּוֹב
אוּלַי חָטְאוּ בָנַי
וּבֵרְכוּ אֱלֹהִים בִּלְבָבָם

(1:5a)

Here, the verb ברכו, literally "blessed", has the opposite meaning, that is, blasphemed, cursed, (see also ברך in verses 11; 2:5, 9, and in I Kings 21:10, 13; Psalm 10:3). Critical commentators see in this usage of ברך a later emendation in favor of euphemistic language; the traditional commentators see it as a euphemism which was used in the original text out of reverence for God. Examination of the story's complex composition reveals that in this case the received text (בֵּרְכוּ, יְבָרְכֶךָ, בָּרֵךְ) is indeed the original, and that the verb ברך serves in its two antithetical meanings, to bless and to curse.

Job trusted his sons' righteousness. He was confident that even during a seven-day feast, their hearts merry with wine, they had not sinned. In this, too, his joy was complete; he knew that his sons followed in his footsteps. Yet this trust in his sons' fear of sin did not lead to complacency. On the contrary, his reverence allowed for no respite in his service of God. Job was innocent, but he was not naive; he was תם, not תמים, not unaware of the existence of evil. Even in his innocence he knew of the ways of man, that "great is man's wickedness on earth, and every plan devised by his mind is nothing but evil all the time" (Genesis 6:5). But, although where the fear of God was concerned he was strict with his sons, he never had even the shadow of a doubt that they sinned in deed or even in word. His only apprehension was that they had sinned "in their *heart*", where man has no control. And even this was but a minute suspicion: "it *may be* that my sons have sinned". It is odd that, on the one hand Job's apprehension should be so slight, and on the other, that his fear concerned the greatest sin of all, blasphemy. But this detail, too, serves to portray Job's conscientiousness and remarkable sense of responsibility, to stress how seriously he took the service of God. Bringing offerings to atone for his sons' most hypothetical sin did not ease his conscience. Not only did he bring offerings "one for each of them", but he sacrificed them with the intention of atoning for the most serious sin of all.

Thus Job did continually. *(1:5b)* כָּכָה יַעֲשֶׂה אִיּוֹב כָּל־הַיָּמִים

The *yiqtol* form of the verb expresses a repetitive action: this was his regular habit. That Job's meticulous piety is innate to his character is demonstrated by the fact that in the first part of our story, apart from the sentence אִיּוֹב שְׁמוֹ ("Job was his name"), which is a parenthetical expression, it is only in this last sentence describing his actions that Job's name appears. And, for no informative purpose, the name Job appears in three consecutive clauses: "And Job sent", "for Job said", "thus Job did".

The episode related in verses 4-5 serves to illustrate what was previously only implied. In the first account, which simply states the facts, Job's righteousness is mentioned first and then the result of that righteousness, its reward; in the narration which describes the facts, it is first Job's circumstances in life that are depicted, and afterwards, as a sort of explanation and justification, his strict fear of God. This is the image which concludes the first scene. Against the backdrop of Job's absolute righteousness we proceed to Scene II.

Scene II
(1:6-12)

One day, the sons of God came to present themselves before the LORD, and Satan too came along with them.

(1:6)

וַיְהִי הַיּוֹם וַיָּבֹאוּ בְּנֵי הָאֱלֹהִים
לְהִתְיַצֵּב עַל־ה'

וַיָּבוֹא גַם־הַשָּׂטָן בְּתוֹכָם

A moment ago, at the end of verse 5, we read "thus Job did continually (כל הימים literally, "all the days"), and now, at the beginning of verse 6, we are told of what occurred "one day", one of the days referred to in כל הימים "all the days", not in the Land of Uz but in heaven. We were in the Land of Uz, watching Job arise at dawn in order to offer sacrifices and to send for his children, and now we are in heaven watching how "the sons of God came to present themselves before the LORD". At the conclusion of the earthly scene, Job stood alone on the stage; of his children we heard only that they were summoned. At the opening of the heavenly scene we see both the "sons of God" and the LORD. Of the "sons of God" it is clearly stated that they came; God's presence is mentioned only indirectly. While it is implied that the "sons of God" stand at attention before the LORD, we know nothing of God's position except for the inference that, in contrast to the "sons of God", God Himself is to be perceived here as sitting. The scene before us is that of a divine assembly, a concept that was widespread in the ancient Near East. In the Ugaritic epic, and in Psalm 82 which it probably influenced, the assembly is referred to as עדת אל "the assembly of God". This heavenly scene reproduces the scene on earth of a king seated on his throne surrounded by his court: ministers, servants and subjects. In the Bible, this scene is not merely mentioned, (see also Isaiah 6), it is also depicted (I Kings 22: 19 and Daniel 7:9-10). The vision of Micaiah ben Yimla (I Kings 22) resembles most closely the scene in our story: "I saw the LORD sitting on His throne, and all the host of heaven standing by Him on His right and on His left" (I Kings 22:19). The similarity of the two portrayals is significant, but since we are interested not in their literary interdependence but in what our story represents, we have to focus rather on the differences between the two scenes.

In the story of Micaiah ben Yimla, we read of כל צבא השמים "all the host of Heaven"; in our story of the בני האלהים "sons of God". Much has been written on the origin of this expression, on its earlier and later meanings and those of its synonym בני אלים "sons of gods" (Psalm 29:1; 89:7).[9] In our case, the "sons of God" are beings belonging to God's entourage; they are called "sons" of God in the same way that the members of a prophetic band are called "sons" of the prophets (בני הנביאים) and those who belong to a company of gatekeepers, apothecaries, etc., are called "sons" of gatekeepers (בני השוערים, Ezra 4:2) and "sons" of apothecaries (בני הרקחים, Nehemiah 3:8), etc. The "sons of God", then, are to be identified with those figures usually referred to in the Bible as מלאכים "messengers" (or "angels", from the Greek word for

9. See M. D. Cassuto, אנציקלופדיה מקראית in: "בני אלים, בני (ה)אלהים, בני עליון, II, Jerusalem 1954, pp. 172-174.

messengers), or, in the story of Micaiah ben Yimla, as the "host of Heaven". If this is the case, why are they called by the unusual name "sons of God" and not by the more conventional מלאכים "messengers" when in our story they come "to present themselves before the LORD"? Apparently because the literal meaning of מלאך is "agent", "emissary"; heavenly beings in the Bible are called מלאכים only when they are spoken of specifically as fulfilling a mission on behalf of God and in our story the בני אלהים are not emissaries. But why does the appellation used here differ from its counterpart in I Kings 22, which offers so many parallels to our story, and yet employs the expression צבא השמים "host of Heaven"? The explanation lies in the respective contexts of the two expressions. Each is used as a function of different thematic considerations. The purpose of the story of Micaiah ben Yimla would not be served in its entirety were those who stood before God "on His right and on His left" called by the name "sons of God", and the effect or our story of Job would similarly be lessened were those who came "to present themselves before the LORD" called the "host of Heaven". In the expression "sons of God" there is a sense of intimacy, if individuality, that does not exist in the more general, collective expression "host of Heaven". This difference derives from the distinct nature of each story. The description in the story of Micaiah ben Yimla is intended to be a glorious, prophetic vision; the description in Job is part of a story whose aspect is altogether more intimate. This distinction is conveyed also in the fact that in I Kings 22 God puts His question to the entire "host of Heaven", whereas in Job God turns to one of the individuals present and puts His question to him alone. Likewise, in I Kings the question asked is to the point; here, the first question is purely formal. Everything is determined by the ambience of the celestial scene, which parallels that of the earlier scene on earth: this is the key to understanding the meaning and purpose of the two celestial scenes, and the names used to denote the heavenly entourages.

It has been pointed out that the celestial scene in the story of Micaiah ben Yimla is a reflection of the events taking place on earth. God sits upon His throne and all the host of heaven stand before Him; on earth, the two kings are on their thrones "in a threshing floor in the entrance of the gate of Samaria, the assembly of prophets standing and prophesying before them" (I Kings 22:10). And the wind that steps forth from among the "host of heaven" (verse 21) corresponds to Zedekiah ben Chenaanah among the prophets (verse 11).[10] These parallels reveal Micaiah ben Yimla's intention, namely, to indicate ironically that Zedekiah ben Chenaanah does indeed speak in God's name, but only as the tempting spirit of falsehood. Likewise, in the description of the heavenly scene in our story, one can discern the basic images that are present in the earthly scene. At the close of the earthly scene, we saw Job meticulously serving God; at the opening of the heavenly scene we see God defending Job's honor. On earth the sons of Job are summoned; in heaven the "sons of God" appear. Thus not only is the portrayal of the scene in heaven juxtaposed with that of the scene in the Land of Uz, thereby accentuating the correlation between the two worlds, but in addition, the scenes are described in parallel terms. This correlation is not simply aesthetic, it is also expressive, as is the description of the heavenly scene and the scene in the gate of Samaria in I Kings 22.

One might counter the above view with the claim that the "Satan" who appears in the celestial scene (6b-12) has no parallel on earth. At first sight this may appear to be true, but in fact the character of Satan in our story does reflect one of the earthly events described previously. This becomes clear when one examines the narrator's use of the word "Satan". It is not sufficient to investigate the origin of Satan in ancient eastern mythology and contemporary folklore, or to discuss the role played by Satan or by similar figures in the writings of pre-biblical civilizations, in post-biblical Jewish sources, or even in other portions of the Bible itself, as scholars have usually done (in the course of debate on the authenticity of Satan in our story). Although these elucidations might shed light on matters outside the story, they do not pertain to the story in question, nor do they reveal the particular meaning with which our author has invested the image of Satan. For even were it to be proven that Satan is not an *original* part of the story, he is nonetheless an *integral* part of the story in its extant form. Whoever introduced the figure of Satan into the story also endowed him with a specific meaning that is yet to be discovered: this is the task of exegesis. Nonetheless, we must still investigate the linguistic origin of the name "Satan" and inquire into the origin of the concept and the additional biblical uses of the image. In order to make a precise and comprehensive examination, due attention

---

10. I. L. Seeligmann, "לבעיות הנבואה בישראל, תולדותיה ואופיה", *Eretz Israel*, III, Jerusalem 1954, p. 127.

should be given to Satan's speech and actions as they appear in the story, as regards content, style and structure.

The word שטן occurs in the Bible as both noun and verb. Opinion differs as to whether the verb שטן is derived from the noun or the noun from the verb, the verb being synonymous with שטם "to hate", "to speak evil of". The use of the noun שטן in the Bible is not consistent. There are three different usages, reflecting three stages in the semantic development of the word:

1) Speaking of David, the Philistine princes say to Achish. "Let him not go down with us to battle, lest in the battle he be לשטן (an adversary) to us" (I Samuel 29:4); David says "What have I to do with you, you sons of Zeruiah, that you should today be לשטן (an adversary) to me?" (II Samuel 29:13). Here שטן is not a proper noun, nor is it an appellation or an adjective, the bearer of which discharges a specific function. Rather, it is an indication of behavior or of a trait that leads to a certain type of behavior. He who opposes is לשטן, the adversary of the opposed. And at times the adversary is simply called שטן without the preposition ל, as when Solomon sends word to Hiram "But now the LORD my God has given me rest on all sides, אין שטן ואין פגע רע so that there is neither adversary nor evil hindrance" (I Kings 5:18). Here the word שטן "adversary" is used in conjunction with פגע רע "evil hindrance", meaning opposition, trouble in general. Moreover, in the verse "The LORD stirred up an adversary (שטן) to Solomon, Hadad the Edomite" (I Kings 11:14; compare 23:25), the reference is to a political opponent, as it is in the words of the psalmist "Set a wicked man (רשע) over him; and let an adversary (שטן) stand at his right hand" (Psalm 109:6); שטן is parallel to רשע, one who opposes justice. An angel, too, by opposing someone, may become a שטן to that person, as can be inferred from the story of Balaam: "The angel of the LORD placed himself in his way לשטן as an adversary". Further on, the angel says to Balaam "It is I who came out לשטן as an adversary . . . " (Numbers 22:22, 32). From this usage we can also determine that the behavior indicated by the word שטן is not in itself objectively evil. Here, as in the other instances mentioned, the word שטן indicates an attitude of opposition, occasional and transient, caused by a specific, temporary situation.

2) In Zachariah we read: "He showed me Joshua the high priest standing before the angel of the LORD, and השטן the adversary was

standing at his right לשטנו to thwart him. And the LORD said to the adversary. 'The LORD rebukes you, השטן O adversary...'" (Zachariah 3:1-2). Here השטן is the prosecutor, an officer in the employ of God. His role is directly derived from his nature: to prosecute, to bring to justice. In this vision, therefore, the word השטן does not indicate a temporary state but a permanent office; for this reason it is prefixed by the definite article.

3) "And שטן Satan arose against Israel and incited David to number Israel" (I Chronicles 21:1). The precise meaning of the word שטן as used here becomes clear when one considers the corresponding verse in Samuel "Again *the anger of the LORD* burned against Israel, and *He* incited David against them, saying, 'Go, number Israel and Judah'" (II Samuel 24:1). In the Book of Samuel it is God that incites David; in Chronicles it is Satan. In Chronicles, unlike Zachariah and Job, the word has no definite article; it is not a common noun but a proper noun, denoting the heavenly being who incites and tempts human beings to sin so that God will punish them. Hence a noun used to indicate a temporary state of opposition became the term for an office in heaven – the prosecutor in the celestial court. From here we continue to the next and final stage, where Satan is the proper name of a celestial personage who incites men against God. The word שטן which we found in the third stage is used in later demonology as well as in a few of the apocryphal works, and — especially — in the New Testament. Basically, this is also the concept of the שטן as expressed in the *baraitha:* "He descends and leads men astray, then ascends and moves God to anger" (*Talmud Bab., Baba Batra* 16a).

The author of our story uses the image of Satan as it is used in the vision of Zachariah, hence the parallel use of the definite article. The conceptual similarity is indicated by the fact that in Zachariah, the Satan prosecutes, but his behavior and his opposition are not objectively evil: he is the prosecutor, but not the informer, the *diabolos,* as the word שטן is translated in the Septuagint (hence the Indo-European names: *diable* in French, devil in English, *Teufel* in German). True, he "opposes", though not in a spirit of malice, but rather because he meticulously clings to justice, on the principle "Let justice be done though the heavens fall". After all, Joshua the high priest (Zachariah 3) was in fact guilty: he was dressed in garments covered with excrement, and he himself donned them in his guilt. Satan did not garb him in foul clothes through an unjust accusation. The garments are removed when God forgives his sin: he is acquitted not through justice, but through mercy, through pardon, "for this man is a brand plucked out of the fire" (Zachariah 3:2) — God grants him immunity from prosecution. The same happens in the story of Job. When Satan takes leave of God in order to destroy Job's possessions, and later on to harm Job himself, it is on God's authority that he tests Job. What he does may be evil from Job's point of view, but not from God's, for it is done with His sanction. When Satan argues against Job before God, his opposition is perhaps that of a prosecutor, but it would be more accurate to consider it as an expression of mistrust. Can it be said of Satan in our story that his objections are a result of outright hatred? Is not his hostility to Job, like his hostility to Joshua the high priest in Zachariah, based on devotion to principle? Does he not merely insist on the truth, and therefore suspect even the innocent, precisely because he believes that there are no blameless men and that Job, therefore, cannot be blameless either?

This question has to be answered. In fact, Satan's very nature in our story is an issue that requires clarification, since it involves a number of unusual points. In the narrator's remarks on Satan, he conceals more than he reveals. It is clear from the story that Satan is one of the "sons of God". He is, therefore, subordinate to God. At the same time, he disagrees with God. And although God's view differs from that of Satan, God does not oppose Satan's suggestion but agrees to it without hesitation. The second time, he gives His full agreement immediately, even though He has already proclaimed to Satan "You incited me against him to destroy him without cause" (2:3). Are God's words not surprising? Perhaps Rabbi Yochanan was correct in observing "Were it not written in the Bible, it would be impossible to say: God is like a man whom someone tries to incite and who is in the end incited" (*Talmud Bab., Baba Batra* 16a). The author of our narrative takes the same view of Satan as Zachariah does: he regards Satan as the "leader of the opposition" in the celestial assembly. But while in Zachariah God rebukes Satan for opposing Him and Satan disappears, in Job God rebukes Satan for inciting Him — and He is indeed incited — while at the same time allowing Himself to be incited yet again. What did the narrator see in his Satan? What role did he assign him? Why did he portray the relationship between God and Satan as one that contradicts the relationship between authority and subordination? These problems will not be resolved, nor will the nature of

an in our story be determined, until we account for the use of the word
'. First, then, we have to explain why שטן is used at all to refer to a
heavenly being.

As we have seen, the name שטן is related to a heavenly being even in
its original usage: in the story of Balaam, שטן is used to indicate the
angel's attitude of opposition to Balaam. The verse reads: "God's anger
was aroused at his going, so the angel of the LORD placed himself in His way as an adversary" (Numbers 22:22). While
the subject of the first clause is God's anger, the subject of the second is
the angel. The juxtaposition of God and His angel is not unusual in
biblical narrative; for example, "And God heard the voice of the lad, and
the angel of God called to Hagar" (Genesis 21:17); "God tested
Abraham ... and an angel of the LORD called to him from heaven"
(Genesis 22:1, 11); "An angel of the LORD appeared to him ... and
when the LORD saw that he turned aside to look ... " (Exodus 3:2, 4);
"Then Manoah knew that he was an angel of the LORD. And Manoah
said to his wife, we shall surely die, because we have seen God" (Judges
13:21-22). The interchanging of God and His angel reflects the idea that
God's emotions, thoughts, will, speech, and action are made known to
mankind not by God Himself but through His angel. The angel is nothing
more than a manifestation of God Himself. God's objection to Balaam's
mission is not expressed by God appearing in person "in his way as an
adversary", but through the offices of an angel of God. The consistency
of this phenomenon, confirming its significance as a feature of style, is
evidenced in I Chronicles 21, where the inciting of David to take a
national census is attributed not to God Himself, as in the parallel account in II Samuel 24, but to Satan. It would appear that the account in
Chronicles was made to accord with the belief that God does not tempt
man to sin in order to punish him. What is done by God Himself in the
first account is done by Satan in the alternative version, just as it was
God's anger that was aroused against Balaam, and yet Balaam's "satan"
was not God, but His angel.

There is, however, an essential difference between the action of Satan
in Chronicles and that of the angel when he appears as Balaam's adversary. In the story of Balaam, the angel's action is in fact God's action; the
appearance of an angel is God's own appearance as a "satan". For here,
as we have mentioned, the angel does not possess an independent per-

sonality; he is but a shadow of the transcendent God. The Satan in Chronicles, however, is an independent agent who does whatever he pleases, even in opposition to God. Here Satan is not an image of God but the embodiment (hypostasis[11]) of opposition to God's will. Substituting "angel of God" for "God" in the story of Balaam is a purely formal device, while in the story of the census in Chronicles, replacing God by Satan as "provocateur" is a real change of subject, in fact an emendation of the original account given in II Samuel. In both the prophecy of Zachariah and the story of Job, Satan is an independent personality, an entity in himself, who has a mind of his own. Here, then, he is a hypostasis. But although he objects to God's opinion, he does not oppose His will. When God rebukes him, the holds his peace and disappears; only when God grants His consent does he act. Therefore the image of Satan in our story is an intermediate concept between those reflected, respectively, in the story of Balaam and in the story of David.

Furthermore, in Zachariah and in Job, Satan is indeed a hypostasis — not of actual opposition to God, however, but of one of the contradictory, ambivalent traits of God Himself. In the vision of Zachariah, Satan embodies the truth that God abounds in kindness. Instead of God being revealed as compassionate, gracious and forgiving, yet at the same time not remitting punishment and visiting the iniquity of fathers upon children (see Exodus 34:6-7), here He is only merciful, while His other attribute, that of justice, is personified in Satan. This is similar to Satan's role in Job: whereas in the story of Isaac, it was God who tested Abraham (Genesis 22:1), that is, God Himself needed to ascertain Abraham's complete faithfulness, even though He is conceived as understanding the depths of the heart (for this reason it is the angel who later says "Now I know that you fear God", verse 12), in our story God is certain and convinced of Job's steadfast righteousness, while doubt, expressed in the desire to put Job to the test, is attributed to Satan.

From this we may conclude that in both Zachariah and Job, the use of the word שָׂטָן is a result of theological considerations. In Zachariah the prophet wished to illustrate the notion that God is actuated only by His quality of mercy; here, the story-teller sought to preclude the notion that

---

11. Hypostasis: perception of a particular characteristic or emanation of the Divine as a divinity itself, as an independent entity, or as a personification of one of God's attributes.

He who is all-knowing can have any doubt. This assumption concerning the narrator's motive, which offers a solution to all the difficulties in the description of Satan, is confirmed by both the wording and the structure of the heavenly scene. In his vision, Zachariah is placed opposite God, and in the midst of the divine entourage are the "angel of God" and "the Satan". The angel of God does not defend Joshua against Satan the prosecutor, as would usually be the case, rather the defender is God Himself, and the angel only executes the pardon granted by God to Joshua delivering God's word to him. Hence the role of the angel is the same as in those stories in which God and the angel appear interchangeably. In our story, only God is described as being present from the start; His entourage is indicated as having come later. The "sons of God" are only supernumeraries; they play no role. They come to present themselves before God (1:6). The belief of most commentators that the sons of God appear in order to give an accounting before God and to receive orders from Him has no basis in the text. The verb התיצב expresses only the action of appearing (Deuteronomy 31:14; Judges 20:2; etc.). The "sons of God" come only to appear, to present themselves before God, and no more.

All the details of this description support the assumption that the celestial scene in the story is intended to reflect the earthly scene depicted earlier. Above, God alone is present at first, just as there was only Job on earth. The "sons of God" come only to present themselves before God, just as the sons of Job were sent for in order to be present with Job. Of course, for the parallel to be complete there would have to be some heavenly analogy not only to Job's calling for his sons but also to his doing so in consequence of his doubt, as a father so concerned about his sons' righteousness. Indeed, this detail is also to be found; however, in view of the theological consideration already mentioned, the story-teller did not embody the doubt in God Himself, but in the image of Satan. Thus in this heavenly being, too, is reflected a detail from the events on earth. Satan is the heavenly counterpart to Job's apprehension concerning his sons' conduct. Satan's words to God "He will *blaspheme* You (יברכך) to Your face" (verse 11) echo Job's thought "it may be that my sons have sinned and *blasphemed* (וברכו) God in their hearts" (verse 5).

This provides the key to the full implication of "and גם השטן Satan *too* came along with them" (verse 6b). At first sight, it is unclear whether the

40

word גם ("too", "also") is meant to indicate that Satan *too* was among the "sons of God", or that he *too*, like them but not as one of them, came to present himself before God. If the above assumption is correct, then Satan also came, as did the "sons of God", but not, like them, in order to present himself before God, since he is no more than the embodiment of God's apprehension. The phrasing of the verse lends credence to this theory: in contrast to what is written later, "Satan, too, came along with them to stand before God" (2:1), here we read "Satan, too, came along with them". Further, while the "sons of God" have a purpose in appearing right from the outset (to present themselves before God), the appearance of Satan is given a purpose by God only later on, when God speaks to him. In fact, the appearance of Satan is brought about only as a result of the appearance of the sons of God. If Job's invitation to his sons to be present with him was a result of his apprehension, it would stand to reason that in the heavenly parallel of this scene the arrival of the "sons of God" is what prompts God's apprehension. And so it is: first, "The sons of God came to present themselves before the LORD", then, "Satan, too, came along with them".

Our idea of Satan's function is reflected in his dialogue with God. This will be clearer if we compare the beginning of the dialogue with another story, evidently influenced by ours, found in the book of Jubilees and concerning the trial of Abraham: "And the minister Mastema came before God and said: Behold Abraham loves his son Isaac and he has given him everything. Tell him to sacrifice him upon the altar, and see if he will do it. Then You will know whether he is faithful under any test You may give him" (Jubilees 17:15). According to this story, the opening statement is made by Mastema, that is, Satan (from the root שטמ "to hate", "to speak evil of", see above, p. 35). Similarly, in rabbinic homilies which speak of the sacrifice of Isaac, it is either the "satan" or the "ministering angels" who open the discussion. In our story God does so. In the extra-biblical stories that speak of the trial of Abraham, the dialogue between God and either Satan or the angels comprises only two steps: each of the two participants speaks but once. In our story, God speaks three times and Satan twice. His first is strictly a formality:

The LORD said to Satan,	וַיֹּאמֶר ה' אֶל־הַשָּׂטָן
"Where are you coming from?"	מֵאַיִן תָּבֹא

(1:7a)

41

It is only Satan's response that evokes God's second, more important question:

The LORD said to Satan,	וַיֹּאמֶר ה׳ אֶל הַשָּׂטָן
"Have you observed my servant Job,	הֲשַׂמְתָּ לִבְּךָ עַל עַבְדִּי אִיּוֹב
that there is no one like him on earth,	כִּי אֵין כָּמֹהוּ בָּאָרֶץ
a blameless and upright man,	אִישׁ תָּם וְיָשָׁר
who fears God and shuns evil?" *(1:8)*	יְרֵא אֱלֹהִים וְסָר מֵרָע

The variation in the structure of the dialogue indicates not only the artistic superiority of our story but also deeper psychological insight, for the structure reveals a struggle taking place. In order to view this struggle correctly, we must examine the wording. God's opinion of Job is expressed in a question and not as a declarative statement. It cannot be claimed a priori that this structure is merely a technical device which allows Satan's reaction to be given in the form of an answer, or that it serves only the aesthetic purpose of animating the dialogue; one must first assume that the use of the interrogative is also (perhaps mainly) an expressive device, calling our attention to the fact that Job's righteousness, so unequivocally postulated, is here being called into question. Formally, the question is put by God to Satan, but is Satan really being asked? Although, as we said, the structure of the dialogue would seem to indicate a struggle between God and Satan, neither style nor content betray any trace of conflict! Satan proposes, and God immediately agrees with him. In fact, as we shall see in our treatment of verse 12, God even authorizes Satan to do more than he had originally suggested. Does not this remarkable circumstance confirm the hypothesis that Satan's reply to God's question was the answer that God Himself required? We have already mentioned that this dialogue is characterized by a sense of intimacy: there is certainly no reverential tone apparent in the words addressed to God, and Satan's speech is not that of a servant to his master, nor are God's words to Satan those of master to servant. Does this not indicate that questioner and questioned, answered and answerer are in fact one and the same? That the "dialogue" between God and Satan is in truth a monologue, a discussion between God and Himself, God's own internal conflict?

42

The storyteller thus correlates the heavenly scene with the earthly scene, not only by juxtaposing the two scenes without any transition, but also by constructing the description of the heavenly occurrences from constituents analogous to those which comprise the depiction of events in the Land of Uz. This indicates the story's perception of the heavenly debate and its results as a reaction to Job's way of life and his fortune on the earthly scene. Job's way of life: the life of perfect righteousness. His fortune: perfect bliss. So it is, for "Job was his name". So it has to be, for he dwells "in the Land of Uz", in a land whose religious world is built on the principle of recompense for the righteous. Job is righteous, therefore blessed. He has faith in his righteousness, as in his sons' righteousness, and only "when the cycle of feast days was complete" does there arise within him the shadow of a doubt. And in order that he might continue even then to have complete faith in his sons, he "arose early in the morning to offer burnt offerings, one for each of them." In this he places his trust; on this he relies.

However, this faith of the Land of Uz is dangerous. There exists within it the concept of *do ut des*, I will give in order to receive. It is a foolish, even pagan, attitude, and it is wholly misconceived. The aim of our story is to show that the world of "the Land of Uz", the world of the doctrine of Wisdom, stands upon a false foundation. To destroy this world and to build upon its ruins a world of truth — this is the intention of the story, this is the meaning of the juxtaposition of the two worlds, the Land of Uz below, where Job lives, and the heavens above, where God dwells. In order to destroy the world of the Land of Uz, the home of the righteous Job must be destroyed, together with all that he has, and in order to build a world of truth, it must first be seen how Job will react when reality delivers an unexpected blow. Therefore it is not sufficient to compare Job's fidelity to God's trust in him. It is also necessary that, corresponding to Job's apprehension and to his faith in his ability to dispel that apprehension, there appear "Satan's" (i.e. God's) apprehension and God's agreement to Satan's suggestion. Job, when apprehensive, offers sacrifices, summons his sons, and is confident that all suspicions have been dismissed and all errors corrected. In contradistinction and in contradiction, God tells Satan to lay his hand on all that Job owns: will he become a different person if the "Land of Uz" suddenly reverses itself? Will he remain steadfast in the face of occurrences that in his spiritual

43

world would be considered a distortion? This is the question that is
vividly posed and presented in the form and content of the the first two
sections of the story, as we have seen in our survey of both scenes and as
we shall see further in our detailed examination of the second scene.

The dialogue begins with God's address to Satan. If it is God's intention to discuss Job's righteousness, then this matter must be on His mind.
To open the conversation, He asks מאין תבא "Where are you coming
from?" (1:7). The verb תבא is in the imperfect, not, as in the angel's question to Hagar, אי מזה באת "Where have you come from" (Genesis 16:8).
Both questions refer to an action already complete: the perfect implies an
action completed in the past, the imperfect an action at its moment of
completion. The precise interpretation of God's question is: where are
you coming from just now?

Satan answered the LORD,	וַיַּעַן הַשָּׂטָן אֶת־ה' וַיֹּאמַר
"From roaming back and forth over the earth	מִשּׁוּט בָּאָרֶץ
and from walking about there."	וּמֵהִתְהַלֵּךְ בָּהּ

(1:7b)

From the point of view of information, the first part of Satan's answer
"from roaming back and forth over the earth" is interchangable with the
second part "and from walking about there". But in the first phrase משוט
בארץ there is also an intentional word-play on the verb שוט and the noun
שטן. This play on words does not, of course, indicate the original meaning
of the name Satan (as Luzzatto and Tur-Sinai claim); rather, it illustrates
the idea that he is what his name implies. When Satan responds to God's
question "Where are you coming from" with the answer משוט בארץ, we
infer: I have come from fulfilling my task, the task implied by my name. I
am the שטן, the doubting, suspicious one; therefore I roam (שט) about the
earth. Satan roams the earth just as the eyes of God roam the earth (II
Chronicles 15:9; Zachariah 4:10) — another hint, perhaps, that Satan is
a hypostasis of an attribute of God?

God's principal question comes as a reaction to Satan's answer:

The LORD said to Satan,	וַיֹּאמֶר ה' אֶל־הַשָּׂטָן
"Have you observed My servant Job,	הֲשַׂמְתָּ לִבְּךָ עַל עַבְדִּי אִיּוֹב

44

that there is no one like him	כִּי אֵין כָּמֹהוּ בָּאָרֶץ
on earth	
a blameless and upright man,	אִישׁ תָּם וְיָשָׁר
who fears God and shuns evil?"	יְרֵא אֱלֹהִים וְסָר מֵרָע

(1:8)

In other words, God asks, since you have come from roaming about the earth, Satan, you the opponent, the doubter, the suspicious one, have you noticed my servant Job? Is there still room for suspicion or doubt, since there is no one like him on earth? Satan, however, does not answer God's question, instead he takes up the characterization of Job as one who fears God:

Satan answered the LORD,	וַיַּעַן הַשָּׂטָן אֶת־ה' וַיֹּאמַר
"Does Job fear God for nought?"	הַחִנָּם יָרֵא אִיּוֹב אֱלֹהִים

(1:9)

His answer is a question of double significance: it is a question which requires an answer, and at the same time it is a rhetorical question containing its own answer; that is, it is both an expression of doubt and an expression of certainty. There is in Satan's question no rejection, nor even any doubt, of God's claim that Job is God-fearing. His question is "Does Job fear God *for nought?*" Does Job serve God without reward, and not, rather, in order to receive reward?

And to emphasize his words he adds:

"Have You not fenced him about,	הֲלֹא־אַתָּ שַׂכְתָּ בַעֲדוֹ וּבְעַד־בֵּיתוֹ
him and his household and all	וּבְעַד כָּל־אֲשֶׁר־לוֹ מִסָּבִיב
that he has?"	

(1:10a)

That is, You have surrounded his house with a hedge, You have enclosed it in a fence of thorns, so that whoever even draws near is pricked. Satan places special emphasis on God's supreme protection of Job by adding the pronoun "You" (את), normally omitted in the verbal sentence in Hebrew, as if to say, Are You not the One who has fenced him about? He also states:

You have blessed the work of his hands	מַעֲשֵׂה יָדָיו בֵּרַכְתָּ

so that his possessions spread
out in the land."

וּמִקְנֵהוּ פָּרַץ בָּאָרֶץ

(1:10b)

That is, his cattle multiply so quickly that they exceed all limits; there is
no fence capable of containing his herds. Satan thus illustrates his conten-
tion that Job fears God for good reason by pointing out two contradictory manifestations of God's blessing. In order to discover whether Job's
fear of God is indeed without expectation of recompense, Satan suggests
to God:

"But put forth Your hand
and touch whatever he has,
then will he not blaspheme
You to Your face?"

וְאוּלָם שְׁלַח־נָא יָדְךָ
וְגַע בְּכָל־אֲשֶׁר־לוֹ
אִם־לֹא עַל־פָּנֶיךָ יְבָרְכֶךָּ

(1:11)

"Whatever he has", meaning anything of his, as is implied by the verb עג
"touch", which refers to contact with the very edge of the object. As long
as the present situation exists, Satan claims, as long as You have blessed
the work of his hands, Job fears You. But the moment You put out Your
hand and even touch something of his, then he will "blaspheme You to
Your face". Either bless the work of his hands, or he will "bless" — i.e.
blaspheme — You. The sentence אם לא על פניך יברכך may be understood
as a rhetorical question ("Will he not . . . ") or as a declarative statement,
in which case the words אם לא are the idiom of oath ("Indeed he will
blaspheme You"). "To Your face" — in public, before everyone; compare Isaiah 65:3. Far worse than what Job suspected of his sons
(blasphemy "in their hearts" [verse 5]), Satan says, Job will blaspheme
You openly, publicly, audaciously.

Satan makes his claim, offers his suggestion, and God, without
demurring and without hesitation, agrees:

The LORD replied to Satan,
"See, all that he has is in
your power"

וַיֹּאמֶר ה' אֶל־הַשָּׂטָן
הִנֵּה כָל־אֲשֶׁר־לוֹ בְּיָדֶךָ

(1:12a)

In fact, although Satan had only proposed that God "touch whatever he has", i.e., merely touch something of his, God says "*All that he has* is in your power".

The dialogue between God and Satan ends in an agreement which has but one condition:

"only do not lay your hand upon him."

רַק אֵלָיו אַל־תִּשְׁלַח יָדֶךָ

(1:12a)

No mention is made of what will become of Satan if his doubts prove to be unfounded. Will he have to keep silent and disappear? If we read the dialogue as has been suggested, as a monologue of God with Himself, then any such concern is out of place and the omission becomes perfectly understandable.

Agreement reached,

Satan left the presence of the LORD.

וַיֵּצֵא הַשָּׂטָן מֵעִם פְּנֵי ה'

(1:12b)

Exit Satan, and the curtain falls on the heavenly scene, only to rise immediately, without intermission, upon the familiar scene on earth.

Scene III
(1:13-22)

One day, as his sons and daughters were eating and drinking wine in their eldest brother's house,

וַיְהִי הַיּוֹם וּבָנָיו וּבְנֹתָיו אֹכְלִים
וְשֹׁתִים יַיִן בְּבֵית אֲחִיהֶם הַבְּכוֹר

(1:13)

Although the content of the verse is clear, the wording is difficult, for while the expression "his sons and daughters" clearly refers to the sons and daughters of *Job*, the possessive "his" appears to follow syntactically upon the subject of the preceding verse, Satan. Scholars consider this proof that the heavenly episode of verses 6-12 is a later interpolation, and that in the original version of the story, the present scene followed after verse 5 and the sentence "Thus Job did continually" was followed by "One day, as his sons and daughters were eating and drinking . . . . " In support of this widely accepted theory, it has been pointed out that the opening phrase of verse 13 ויהי היום "one day" is identical with that of verse 6; this duplication, it is claimed, is a further sign that the section between the two identical phrases is an addition. The repeated phrase, known as resumptive repetition or connecting repetition ("*Wiederaufnahme*"), is a narrative device which is common to biblical literature. It mirrors the phrase that immediately precedes a textual addition, thereby resuming the story. However, the task of exegesis is not to explain the reason for the phenomenon, but rather its meaning; not to determine whether the description of the heavenly scene is *original* to the story, but only whether it is *organic* to the story. Our analysis of Scene II showed that it is indeed an essential part of the story in its present form. This being the case, we cannot ignore the unevenness in the phrasing of verse 12. If we find the unevenness to be of no significance, we must consider it an editorial oversight; but if it has any meaning, then that meaning must be a part of the narrator's plan, contributing to his overall intent.

Looking at verse 13 in its context, we can see that the narrator did not mention *whose* sons and daughters precisely because the omission of Job's name was an appropriate way of indicating that verse 13 is indeed the direct continuation of verse 5, and that the occurrences in heaven in verses 6-12 interrupt the narrative for reasons that are technical, not chronological. Chronologically, verse 13 does not follow verse 12; rather the events in verse 13 and those in verses 6-12 take place simultaneously.[12] The opening phrase common to verses 6 and 13 ויהי היום "one day" is used here (but not in 2:1) as an indication of synchronism.

In order to find support for the theory that the unevenness we detected in verse 13 is intended to signal the continuation of verse 5, let us compare this transition from the heavenly to the earthly scene with that of 2:7. Here, the heavenly scene concludes with "Satan left the presence of

12. Compare the composition technique used here with the editorial device used, for example, in Samuel, where the story of the Philistines' preparations for the decisive battle is interrupted by the account of Saul's visit to the diviner, indicating that the two events occurred simultaneously (I Samuel 28:1-2; 29:1-3).

the LORD" (verse 12), and the earthly scene begins with "One day, as his sons and daughters..." (verse 13). In Chapter 2, however, we read "Satan left the presence of the LORD and inflicted Job with severe sores" (verse 7). In other words, when the scene changes in Chapter 2 and the reader is transported from heaven to earth, the heavenly scene does not end but is transformed into the scene on earth. At the conclusion of 2:7a the curtain does not even fall; rather, the revolving stage goes into motion. In our scene, on the other hand, the curtain falls, at the end of verse 12, and at the beginning of verse 13 it rises. Thus in Chapter 2 the earthly scene is the temporal continuation of the heavenly scene, and the events in heaven and on earth occur consecutively, while in Chapter 1 the earthly scene is the temporal continuation of the previous *earthly* scene, while the heavenly events which are interposed in the text occur concurrently.

As the actors on earth do not know what is taking place in heaven and are therefore unaware of Satan, it would be superfluous to specify the referent of the possessive suffix in "his sons and daughters". As far as the players are concerned, the possessive suffix unmistakeably refers to Job, for he is the subject in the sentence which (for them) precedes our verse, namely, verse 5. Only the reader, who knows of the heavenly scene and recalls that the subject of the phrase preceding verse 13 is Satan, finds the possessive suffix problematic. It is through this very difficulty that the narrator involves the reader in the world of the actors on earth so that he may identify with them as fully as possible.

The second scene on earth thus begins where the first ended. The first earthly scene concluded at the end of the first round of feast days, in the home of the youngest son, and with the sacrifices that Job brought. The second scene opens with the beginning of the second round, with Job's sons and daughters "eating and drinking wine in their eldest brother's house". As we said, placing the second earthly scene in the same spot as the first involves the reader in the world of a Job unaware of what is taking place in heaven. At the same time, this identity of time and location also expresses a dramatic contrast between the two scenes on earth: there where we have just seen Job's greatest happiness, we are about to witness his greatest calamity; we shall behold his sudden fall from the greatest heights to the lowest depths. Furthermore, there where we saw Job in his most exemplary righteousness, blessed with sons and daughters, we shall

49

see him, unchanged in this exemplary righteousness, as a bereaved father. In order to grasp the nature of this steadfastness, one must note that the events in Scene III take place as the sons and daughters are eating and drinking "in their eldest brother's house". If, after seven days of feasting there could not arise — even in the heart of a man like Job, unsurpassed in his fear of God — more than the shadow of a doubt that "it may be that my sons have sinned and blasphemed God in their hearts", then after he offered sacrifices to atone for their hypothetical sin, on the first day of the new round of feasting there surely was no suspicion whatsoever, and Job could be fully certain that his sons were absolutely innocent even of the sin of contemplating blasphemy. And for all that — the catastrophe occurred. And Job, on the very spot and on the very day that he had offered sacrifices out of concern that his sons may have "blessed" (i.e. blasphemed) God, now falls to the earth and says "Blessed be the name of the LORD" (verse 21).

To make the test that Job stands truly difficult, the disasters that befall him are terrible indeed:

[14]a messenger came to Job and said,	וּמַלְאָךְ בָּא אֶל־אִיּוֹב וַיֹּאמַר
"The oxen were plowing and the asses were feeding beside them	הַבָּקָר הָיוּ חֹרְשׁוֹת וְהָאֲתֹנוֹת רֹעוֹת עַל־יְדֵיהֶם
[15]when Sabeans descended and captured them, and put the boys to the sword;	וַתִּפֹּל שְׁבָא וַתִּקָּחֵם וְאֶת־הַנְּעָרִים הִכּוּ לְפִי־חָרֶב
I alone have escaped to tell you."	וָאִמָּלְטָה רַק־אֲנִי לְבַדִּי לְהַגִּיד לָךְ
[16]This one was still speaking when another arrived and said,	עוֹד זֶה מְדַבֵּר וְזֶה בָּא וַיֹּאמַר
"A fire of God fell from heaven,	אֵשׁ אֱלֹהִים נָפְלָה מִן־הַשָּׁמַיִם
took hold of the sheep and the boys and burned them up;	וַתִּבְעַר בַּצֹּאן וּבַנְּעָרִים וַתֹּאכְלֵם
I alone have escaped to tell you."	וָאִמָּלְטָה רַק־אֲנִי לְבַדִּי לְהַגִּיד לָךְ
[17]This one was still speaking when another arrived and said,	עוֹד זֶה מְדַבֵּר וְזֶה בָּא וַיֹּאמַר
"The 'Kasdim' formed three columns and made a raid upon the camels and carried them off,	כַּשְׂדִּים שָׂמוּ שְׁלֹשָׁה רָאשִׁים וַיִּפְשְׁטוּ עַל־הַגְּמַלִּים וַיִּקָּחוּם
and put the boys to the sword;	וְאֶת־הַנְּעָרִים הִכּוּ לְפִי־חָרֶב
I alone have escaped to tell you."	וָאִמָּלְטָה רַק־אֲנִי לְבַדִּי לְהַגִּיד לָךְ

¹⁸This one was still speaking when another arrived and said,

עַד זֶה מְדַבֵּר וְזֶה בָּא וַיֹּאמַר

"Your sons and daughters were eating and drinking wine

בָּנֶיךָ וּבְנוֹתֶיךָ אֹכְלִים וְשֹׁתִים יַיִן

in their eldest brother's house,

בְּבֵית אֲחִיהֶם הַבְּכוֹר

¹⁹and behold, a mighty wind came from across the wilderness.

וְהִנֵּה רוּחַ גְּדוֹלָה בָּאָה מֵעֵבֶר הַמִּדְבָּר

It struck the four corners of the house so that it collapsed upon the young people and they died;

וַיִּגַּע בְּאַרְבַּע פִּנּוֹת הַבַּיִת וַיִּפֹּל עַל־הַנְּעָרִים וַיָּמוּתוּ

I alone have escaped to tell you."

וָאִמָּלְטָה רַק־אֲנִי לְבַדִּי לְהַגִּיד־לָךְ

(1:14-19)

The disasters number four, corresponding to the number of blessings Job had previously enjoyed. They are caused alternately by man and nature: by man — "Sabeans descended upon them and captured them" (verse 15); by nature — "A fire of God fell from heaven" (verse 16); by man — "The 'Kasdim' formed three columns" (verse 17); by nature — "A mighty wind came" (verse 19). The powers above and the powers below are united in the service of Satan to inflict ruin and suffering on Job (Malbim).

The "powers below" are presented by שבא "Sabeans" and "Kasdim". שבא, in southwest Arabia, is considered in the Bible to be the most distant spot on earth (Jeremiah 6:20; Joel 4:8; compare also I Kings 10:1; Psalm 72:10). The provenance of כשדים "Kasdim" in our story is unclear, but they come from afar, from the East. By attributing the raids to Sabeans and "Kasdim", the story seems to be saying that Satan's emissaries of disaster are summoned from the very ends of the earth, from the south and from the east, from the Arabian desert and from the Syrian wilderness. The Sabeans "descended" (ותפל שבא), indicating a sudden, surprise attack; the "Kasdim" "formed three columns", that is, they took pains to plan their attack according to a tried strategy (Judges 7:16, 20; 9:34, 43, 49; I Samuel 11:11; 13:17). In order to overcome an enormous herd of three thousand camels, they divided into three batallions, surrounding and attacking from three sides.

Just as the forces below come from great distances, so too, do the forces above: the fire "from heaven", the wind "from across the wilderness". In order to convey the intended effect, it might have been more fitting that the source of the second natural disaster be the depths of the underworld, to stand in contrast to heaven, but as the underworld is sometimes considered an area over which God has no sovereignty (Psalm 6:6; Isaiah 38:18), a disaster coming from that domain might be regarded as being beyond God's control. The story avoids any such suggestion: Job must not have even the slightest doubt that all the disasters which befall him occur with God's knowledge and consent.

The catastrophe that befalls Job is total. Cruel enough in itself, the effect it has upon him is even more horrifying because of the way in which he learns of it. The catastrophe is especially distressing and the trial especially great since the news reaches Job's ears at a time when he is at peace, in the company of those who are his greatest joy. For the narrator prefaces the account with the line "One day, as his sons and daughters were eating and drinking wine in their eldest brother's house" (verse 13). The meaning of the verse is not the same as that of the parallel verse with which the narrator prefaces the scene in heaven ("One day the sons of God came to present themselves before the LORD" [verse 6]). In the latter verse, the point is to set the stage for what follows; verse 13, however, does not indicate the place of the action, but rather the location of one of the disasters, later to be reported. As to the setting for the action, not even the vaguest hint is given. Where Job actually is does not interest the narrator, for it is of no importance to Job himself. What interests Job is the house of his eldest son, where his sons and daughters are eating and drinking wine; hence this is the detail that is important to the narrator. By opening the scene with the idyllic picture in the home of the eldest son, the narrator places before us the same picture that Job sees, at the moment that the first messenger appears and the plot begins to thicken. It is against this peaceful setting that the narrator presents Job and the messengers.

The messengers' words are phrased uniformly, and their uniformity dramatizes their terrible content. The identical conclusion to each announcement rings with special horror, repeating itself like a refrain: "I alone have escaped to tell you". The repetitive conclusion has greater force than could be attained by any variation, and the line "I alone have escaped to tell you" gives the impression, as it is heard over and over again, that the only reason that these individual boys were saved was so that someone might bring Job the terrible tidings, to cause Job to suffer. This cruel irony contributes to the affliction that has already become unbearable. One report after another comes in; one messenger follows another. Job does not even manage to absorb one catastrophe and the next is already hard upon him: "This one was still speaking when another arrived" (verses 16, 17, 18). In this typical narrative motif, the narrator presents the reader with a messenger, out of breath from running, who has made the journey as quickly as possible to tell his gruesome tale, and waits for the previous messenger to conclude so that he may deliver his own report. Not without reason does the author call the young men who escape to report the tragedies to Job not פליט "refugee" or רץ "courier" but מלאך "messenger". They are emissaries of Satan — in fact, they are collaborators with Satan in the trial. Even unwittingly, perhaps against their will, they add to the pain of Job's trial by the manner in which they announce the tragedies to him.

The first natural disaster is called a "fire of God", which would seem to mean a fire sent by God (see Leviticus 10:2; Numbers 15:35), and this is how it has been understood by the ancient Versions, the Jewish commentators, and some of the moderns. Yet against this interpretation one can argue: a) Had the messenger meant to say that God sent the fire, he would not have used the verb נפלה "fell", and would probably have made God the subject of the sentence; b) The descriptions of all the other disasters announced by the messengers are "secular", and the first disaster is possibly of the same order. It is likely that the messenger is using the word אלהים in one of its applied biblical meanings: in many passages, the name of God, or other divine appellations, appears as a genitive to a preceding construct noun (I Samuel 14:15; 26:12; Isaiah 14:13; Psalm 36:7; Song of Songs 8:6; so too רוח אלהים in Genesis 1:2 according to Radak) as an expression of the superlative. אש אלהים "a fire of God" would then mean the greatest fire. It would seem that this particular idiom was used by the messenger in order to make the effect of the tragedy on Job even more horrifying. Job will automatically hear in this expression the literal meaning of אלהים as well as the idiomatic, even though this is not the meaning intended by the use of the word, and he will think that a violent injustice has been done to him, not only with the knowledge and consent of the LORD but even with His direct personal intervention.

The messenger who brings Job this particular piece of news is not alone in intensifying the trial. For the "coincidental" order in which the messengers arrive, that is, the sequence in which the disasters are reported, seems to have been arranged with the express purpose of maximizing the impact of the calamitous events. This is especially apparent when we compare the sequence of the messengers' reports to that of the blessings recounted by the narrator at the beginning of the story (verses 2-3):

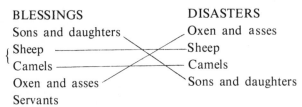

BLESSINGS | DISASTERS
Sons and daughters | Oxen and asses
Sheep | Sheep
Camels | Camels
Oxen and asses | Sons and daughters
Servants

In the description of Job's wealth, the sons and daughters are mentioned first. This is not only the greatest of all of Job's blessings but is also the most essential one. Next, of Job's possessions, the text first mentions two kinds of animals (sheep and camels) that are traditionally the property of a nomad and whose value, because of their low work capacity, is lower than that of the next mentioned pair (oxen and asses), which are standard property of the farmer. Last to be mentioned are the servants, human property whose value is not only in their physical capacity but in their spiritual nature as well. This sequence indicates that after Job was blessed with the most important personal wealth, he was also blessed with material wealth, and not only with animals whose ability to work was negligible but also those of higher work capacity. The list of disasters does not include the loss of servants, for servants are not considered an independent group in everyday life: they are included among the men lost together with the animals with whom they worked. A comparison of the list of disasters with that of blessings shows that while the sheep and camels are mentioned as a pair in the list of blessings, the tidings of their loss are brought separately. This is apparently because the narrator wished the number of disasters to equal the number of blessings, and the loss of "servants", which had been included as a blessing of its own, cannot appear as a separate disaster. And as to the sequence of the disasters, its correspondence to that of the blessings is basically chiastic. In this arrangement, the narrator adopts a construction customary in biblical literature in general. At the same time, it can be said that by adopting a conventional technique and then deviating slightly from it (he mentions the loss of the camels after the loss of the sheep, while according to the chiastic principle he should have mentioned the camels first), he is able to give a psychological basis to the intensification of the trial. First, if Job were to know of the deaths of his sons and daughters from the outset, the announcement of the remaining catastrophes would have been anticlimactic and ineffectual. Therefore the reports of the tragedies begin with the loss of possessions and reach a climax with the death of the children, even though this disaster had certainly taken place in the closest physical proximity to Job and could thus have been reported to him first. Rashi's awareness of the intent behind the sequence of disasters is expressed in his comment on the messengers (on verse 18): "In order to torment him and cause him to sin, Job was told first of his lesser losses and afterward of his greater ones."

Yet careful examination of the sequence of material losses reveals that the narrator does not "recount the misfortune gradually".[13] For the first messenger reports that the most important of the material possessions has been lost — the oxen and the asses — and the second brings the news of the capture of the sheep, whose value as working animals was the least. The third messenger announces the seizure of the camels, which were more important than the sheep but less useful than oxen and asses. Had the sequence proceeded from the least tragedy to the greatest, concluding with the worst of all, the effect would have been less severe; Job's shock would have been cushioned, for he would, to some extent, have become gradually inured to disaster. For this reason he is told first of the greatest material loss, which is followed by a great relief, then by another serious loss, so that the most terrible calamity of all will be felt with its full force.

The first and the last disasters are the most severe, and the gravity of these two worst tragedies is increased by the manner in which the messengers announce them to Job. The style in which the first and last messengers make their reports is identical, as is the style of the second and third. The middle messengers report the tragedies from which they escaped with no introduction: the second opens "A fire of God fell from heaven"; the third, "The 'Kasdim' formed three columns" — they begin

13. As expressed by Ralbag in I Samuel 31:4.

immediately with the description of the catastrophe. But the first messenger begins his report: "The oxen were ploughing and the asses were feeding beside them" (verse 14), and only after evoking the undisturbed scene does he describe the disaster "Sabeans descended" (verse 15). This style is also employed by the last messenger. He begins with "Your sons and daughters were eating and drinking wine in their eldest brother's house" (verse 18) and then goes on to say "a mighty wind came" (v. 19). The stark contrast between the disasters and the serenity that precedes them undoubtedly increases the effect of the two messages upon Job. Moreover, since, of these two greatest disasters, the last is obviously greater than the first, the messenger who announces it intensifies its severity. For while the first messenger magnifies the disaster by beginning with a description of the tranquil scene prior to the onslaught, and proceeds from the idyll directly to the catastrophe without transition, the last messenger, proceeding from the scene of joy to the disaster, begins his announcement with the word והנה: "And behold, a mighty wind came" (verse 19). This addition contributes to the emotional effect, for it increases the tension that Job already feels, particularly since the word והנה is one of emphasis, calling special attention to the announcement which follows. And the impact on the reader is made even greater by the tragic irony in the word והנה, whose effect on Job is not that intended by the messenger: the latter added the exclamation only because he found it difficult to report the death of the sons and daughters, and was trying to gain time, or perhaps in order to cushion the blow that was to follow, on the assumption that even the most terrible news is somewhat less shocking if it is not sprung suddenly. In any case, from what he left out of his message, we can tell that the messenger wished to make things easier for Job. In the announcements given by all four messengers there appears the term הנערים "the boys" (verses 15, 16, 17, 19). In the first three, the word refers to Job's servants. They are called "boys" by the fourth messenger, too, but here the word refers not only to Job's servants but to his children as well. In his description of the happy scene preceding the tragedy, the fourth messenger states specifically: "Your sons and daughters"; when he reports the tragedy itself, he is not emotionally capable of being explicit, so he obscures his meaning by including the sons and daughters in the word הנערים "the boys". Of course, by using this general word, he clearly means to complete his difficult task as quickly as possible, but he certainly also believes that by using the vague term הנערים he will make the tragedy less immediately perceptible than it would have been had he used the words "your sons and daughters".

One final comment regarding the story's manner of describing the catastrophes that befall Job in this first stage of his trial. In biblical narrative, when one character recounts to the others a word or event which the latter have not heard nor seen, the narrator follows one of two paths: a) the event is reported twice, both by the narrator (when it occurs) and by the character himself (when he recounts it to the others); or b) the event is reported only once, either by the narrator or by one of the characters. Our author has chosen the second method to recount the disasters, which means that the reader hears what happened once only, not from the narrator but from the messengers. Although this is a standard technique, the commentator feels compelled to ask why the author chose it over the other. What meaning did he hope to convey by arranging the story so that what happens to Job is made known to the reader not through the narrator but through the messengers? This device requires comment especially in view of the narrator's relationship to the reader up to this point. He has revealed to the reader what is unknown to Job as far as the events in heaven are concerned; but as regards the events on earth, of these the reader learns together with Job. It would appear that the narrator is motivated by didactic considerations both in what he reveals to the reader and in what he conceals. He reveals to the reader what is taking place in heaven for two reasons, one theological, one psychological. The theological point is to inform the reader that what is about to happen to Job is not an injustice on God's part but a trial. (This is also revealed in the first verse of the story of Isaac: "And God tested Abraham" [Genesis 22:1].) The psychological point is to inform the reader of Job's imminent losses and of their purpose, in order to prepare him for what is to come. How will Job, the righteous man, react to events the purpose of which is unknown to him and which, he may deduce according to Wisdom philosophy, constitute a negation of God's righteousness? Afterwards, however, the author conceals from the reader the events taking place on earth because they are not important in themselves, but only as blows that strike Job, as components of the trial which Job must withstand and to which he must react. The reader, like Job, will be informed of the occurrences only by the messengers. The reader will thus experience each blow as a thunderbolt from the blue, as Job does, the swift succession leaving no moment of respite.

When the fourth messenger had concluded his words and Job knew that all was lost,

| Then Job arose, tore his cloak, | וַיָּקָם אִיּוֹב וַיִּקְרַע אֶת־מְעִלוֹ |
| and sheared his head | וַיָּגָז אֶת־רֹאשׁוֹ |

(1:20a)

Rending of the garments, symbolizing pain which rends the heart, is an accepted practice at a time of great sorrow (see Genesis 37:29; 44:13; II Samuel 15:32; Jeremiah 41:5; Esther 4:1). Shaving the head, and other similar acts performed in times of grief, indicates the deviation from social norms that expresses distress (Jeremiah 7:29; 41:5; Micah 1:15; Ezra 9:3). By these reactions Job is only performing socially accepted rites that may indicate religious faith, but may equally be signs of unbelief or despair. Job does not, however, reveal through these acts what is in his own heart. Only in his next act do we see his state of mind:

| and he fell to the ground | וַיִּפֹּל אַרְצָה וַיִּשְׁתָּחוּ |
| and prostrated himself. | |

(1:20b)

Falling earthward and prostrating oneself are no longer expressions of grief, but neither are they in themselves expressions of prayer. They are a sign of surrender prompted by awe (compare Joshua 5:4), a silent testimony to the fact that man accepts what is done to him. Since shaving the head takes time, it would be mistaken to see this as a spontaneous reaction; it is rather a conscious act of submission to the omnipotent decree, though not a verbal submission to the omnipotent Author of the decree. Job fears God, but he is only human. He performs the rites of mourning not only because the social order demands them, but also because he needs them to express his feelings. At first he is able to do so only symbolically. Yet this symbolic action prepares him to arise from his prostration, able to express himself, to verbalize what is in his heart:

| He said, "Naked came I out of | וַיֹּאמֶר עָרֹם יָצָתִי מִבֶּטֶן אִמִּי |
| my mother's womb | |

58

and naked shall I return there;
the LORD gave and the LORD
  has taken away,
blessed be the name of the LORD."

וְעָרֹם אָשׁוּב שָׁמָּה
ה׳ נָתַן וַה׳ לָקָח
יְהִי שֵׁם ה׳ מְבֹרָךְ

(1:21)

The first two sentences are declarative statements; the third, an exclamation, and the three sentences express three different attitudes. The
first is an expression of secular, wordly wisdom, the second conveys
religious meditation, and the third articulates a feeling of faith. In the first
sentence is expressed the awareness of the wise man who sees not only
the outward aspect but also the heart of events. Such a wise man takes an
overall view and argues by analogy. The result of his thinking is: "Naked
came I out of my mother's womb and naked shall I return there." The
word "there" requires explanation. It is obvious that it is not intended
literally, and that the speaker does not conceive of returning to his
mother's womb. Some commentators believe that "there" means into the
earth. This is the viewpoint implied by Ben Sira "From the day he leaves
his mother's womb till the day he returns to the mother of all life" (40:1).
According to this explanation the term "my mother" is ambiguous. In addition to the literal meaning, it also refers figuratively to the concept of
"mother-earth", as in the sentence "I was wrought in the lowest parts of
the earth" (Psalm 139:15). Others believe that the expression "there"
refers to the underworld, as does the word "there" in Job's first
monologue (3:17, 19), and that it is similar to the euphemistic term for the
dead in Egyptian, "existing there", as the underworld is a place that is
only suggested by allusion but not named explicitly. In any case, the
meaning of the sentence "naked shall I return there" is clear: Naked shall
I be brought to the grave. What is stated by Job in this sentence is
similarly expressed in Ecclesiastes (5:14): "As he came out of his
mother's womb, so must he return, naked as he came." Yet despite the
similarity between the two passages, there is a difference; each passage
possesses its characteristic uniqueness. While in Ecclesiastes this statement is an expression of nihilistic resignation, Job is expressing conces-
sion, born of a belief in the unquestionable justification of God's actions.
It is not the weary despair of Ecclesiastes that is expressed in Job's words,
but a strength-giving faith. The declaration which follows is simply the

translation of the first sentence from the language of Wisdom to the language of religion; it is a religious interpretation of the understanding that comes from human experience. The wise man's recognition that man is only temporarily the owner of his possessions induces in Job the awareness of the religious man, that man is *not even temporarily* owner of his possessions, but merely the keeper of a deposit, and for a brief while only. The duration of the deposit is unknown to him, being dependent upon the sovereign will of the Depositor, and when the time comes he will have to return the deposit to its Owner.

This awareness also prompts Job to feel a certain gratitude, the emotion expressed in his third sentence when he exclaims: "Blessed be the name of the LORD". Only now, when Job expresses his reaction as a God-fearing man, does he call God by the Tetragrammaton; elsewhere, throughout the story, he uses the name אלהים — God — which is also the only name used by the narrator when speaking of God in relation to Job, probably because of his desire to present Job as a non-Jew, as in the Bible only Jews call God by the Tetragrammaton. To explain this deviation, which is also a departure from traditional biblical style, scholars have suggested that the author placed in Job's mouth a commonly accepted formula of blessing (part of which appears in Psalm 113:2) without adapting it to the general style and intention of the story.

Job's reaction to the tragedies that befall him has a psychological aspect. Admittedly, Job is described as a man who, as a result of his pure and perfect faith, controls his grief, but he is also portrayed as a man who lived in "the Land of Uz". Through the mechanical observance of rites of mourning, Job relieves his shock somewhat and is able to go through the movements that symbolize his submission to what has befallen him, though he fears God like none on earth. However, as a human being, in order to regain his emotional equilibrium and the strength to express in words his submission to the One who has so dealt with him, he must explain to himself just what has happened to him, and allow his intelligence to check his emotion. And since he is a man from the Land of Uz, that is, a man whose world is that of secular Wisdom which is shaped by the experience of life and speculative inference from life's events, the explanation he gives for his situation must be the sentence "Naked came I out of my mother's womb and naked shall I return there". Only after this rational explanation is he capable of giving another rational explanation, one which derives not from the purely philosophical point of view, but from a religio-philosophical approach: "The LORD gave, the LORD has taken away." These two statements help Job to regain his composure and to arrive at that emotional height at which he has the strength to exclaim "Blessed be the name of the LORD!" Were it not for the two declarative sentences which precede the exclamation, and for the two symbolic acts before them, these words would be no more than lip service. And if Job is indeed using a commonly accepted form of blessing, the blessing would be one pronounced by rote only.

Satan said to God of Job: "Put forth Your hand, and touch whatever he has, and he will *bless* i.e. curse You to Your face". And in truth so it was. The last sentence that Job utters, after all that he owns has been taken from him, is "*Blessed* be the name of the LORD." From this play on the word ברך we may conclude, contrary to accepted theory, that all the verbs of ברך, of "blessing", are original. Just how unfounded Satan's view is, how far he is from knowing Job's soul, cannot be expressed otherwise than ironically, by using the same verb in its two opposite meanings. Satan said of Job "he will *bless* You", literal meaning not intended; and Job said, "*Blessed* be the name of the LORD", literal meaning intended.

Scene III, which presents Job in the first stage of his trial, does not conclude with Job's own words. As in the two previous scenes, the words of the protagonist are followed by the narrator's comment. Just as in the first two scenes, so here, the narrator's observation is superfluous from an informative point of view: there is nothing in it that was not already understood. But these comments have a didactic importance. At the end of the second scene, the narrator's words mark the conclusion of the scene, so that it may be understood not only in the context of the preceding conversation but also in relation to what follows in the third scene, indicating that Scene II is the background against which to understand Scene III. At the conclusion of Scenes I and III, the purpose of the narrator's intervention is to summarize the import of the scene, not only so that we may understand it and not only so that the moral can be made clear, but also to place the moral within our consciousness and to help us to feel the contrast between the earthly scene and the heavenly scene. Therefore, at the conclusion of Job's blessing in verse 21, there comes the appraisal of the author:

For all this, Job did not sin,   בְּכָל־זֹאת לֹא חָטָא אִיּוֹב
nor did he cast reproach on God.   וְלֹא־נָתַן תִּפְלָה לֵאלֹהִים

(1:22)

The word תפלה "reproach", which appears further on in Job (24:12) and also in Jeremiah (23:13), is derived from the root תפל, usually understood in its metaphorical connotation of "to do something useless". According to this explanation, the verse says of Job: "For all this" — all the incomprehensible disasters notwithstanding — "Job did not sin", nor did he attribute meaningless and arbitrary behavior to God.

Scene IV
(2:1-7a)

The description of the second heavenly scene is similar to that of the first — indeed for the most part virtually identical to it:

One day, the sons of God came   וַיְהִי הַיּוֹם וַיָּבֹאוּ בְּנֵי הָאֱלֹהִים
to present themselves before   לְהִתְיַצֵּב עַל־ה׳
   the LORD,
and Satan came along with them   וַיָּבוֹא גַם־הַשָּׂטָן בְּתֹכָם לְהִתְיַצֵּב
to present himself before   עַל־ה׳
   the LORD.

(2:1)

In the Masoretic text, Satan's reason for coming is added: this time it is said not only of the sons of God that they came "to present themselves before the LORD", but of Satan as well. In the Septuagint the verse is identical to 1:6. Most critics see in the Masoretic text's repetition of words from the end of the first half of the verse a dittographic error resulting from a slip of the pen, and they therefore accept the Septuagint as representing the authentic text. Their conclusion can neither be refuted nor confirmed: one cannot discount the possibility that the Masoretic version is a result of a technical error, a result of chance carelessness on the part of the copyist. Yet one must also admit the possibility that the Masoretic version is intentional, that the narrator meant to indicate that this time, unlike the previous instance, Satan had a definite purpose in coming with the sons of God. Admittedly, accepting the Septuagint reading as authentic means that one can explain both that text itself and the origin of the reading in the Masoretic text. But even if one accepts the Masoretic version as authentic, not only can the formation of the Septuagint version be explained, but also the Masoretic text as it stands. Two explanations can be offered for *not* mentioning Satan's purpose in coming, one or both of which may be accepted, depending on how one views the Septuagint version of our book. Perhaps the translator harmonized 2:1b with 1:6b for aesthetic reasons. It is also possible that he altered our verse to conform with its parallel for theological reasons, considering it disrespectful to mention that Satan, coming among the sons of God, came *like them* to present himself before God. And, of course, it is possible that the translator was motivated by both reasons. As for the Masoretic version, this too can be perceived as meaningful. In the first case, Satan's reason for coming is not mentioned while that of the "sons of God" is, since it was the coming of "the sons of God" which prompted Satan to join them. When "the sons of God" came, God recalled a parallel detail in the earthly scene, namely, Job's apprehension, his doubt, which led him to summon his sons and to offer sacrifices. Recalling Job's apprehension in turn led to God's own apprehension, i.e., the appearance of Satan. The "sons of God" came to present themselves, and Satan came only because they did. According to this logic, the narrator mentions this second time that Satan, too, came to present himself, for this time God's doubt was unlikely to arise, since, after all, Job has just said "Blessed be the name of the LORD". The suspicion could not be aroused, for now Job's suspicion "It may be that my sons have sinned" can no longer exist: his sons are no more. In other words, after Job's standing trial has proved that he fears God, and that all the anger of Satan (= God's suspicion) was unfounded, the certainty of that which was in doubt has been shaken. Once it has been proved that Job fears God חנם "for nought", that is, with no expectation of reward, God no longer has any doubt about Job's righteousness. If, in spite of all this, a doubt arose, it did not arise spontaneously, rather, God purposely engendered it, because He desired, in spite of all that happened, that a doubt remain. Consequently, if Satan comes it is not incidental but intentional. It is conceivable, psychologically, that if a suspicion exists it is not the same after the trial as it

was before. Hitherto, it was a spontaneous phenomenon, now it is the
result of considered reasoning. This appears to be so since we read "And
Satan came along with them to present himself before the LORD". If this
assumption is correct, the addition in the Masoretic text is reliable, and
constitutes the only difference between the two descriptions of the
heavenly scenes. Identical depictions would have implied that in the inter-
val between the two scenes, although the world of the man of Uz has been
destroyed, the rest of the world, including the world on high, goes on as
usual. The same is implied by the stereotyped wording of the scene as a
whole:

The LORD said to Satan,	וַיֹּאמֶר ה' אֶל־הַשָּׂטָן
"Where are you coming from?"	אֵי מִזֶּה תָּבֹא
Satan answered the LORD,	וַיַּעַן הַשָּׂטָן אֶת־ה' וַיֹּאמַר
"From roaming back and forth	מִשֻּׁט בָּאָרֶץ וּמֵהִתְהַלֵּךְ בָּהּ
over the earth	
and from walking about there."	

(2:2)

God's words to Satan, when He questions him as if nothing has happened, are also stereotyped, but here, too, a small deviation in style is
significant. God's question is not מאין תבא, but rather אי מזה תבא. As far
as the sense of the words is concerned, both questions are the same, but
the change of wording lends a different tone to the second question, giving
a sense of surprise, perhaps. In any case, Satan answers as before, as if
nothing has happened. God's second question is also like the
corresponding question in the earlier scene:

The LORD said to Satan,	וַיֹּאמֶר ה' אֶל הַשָּׂטָן
"Have you observed My servant Job,	הֲשַׂמְתָּ לִבְּךָ עַל־עַבְדִּי אִיּוֹב
that there is no one like him	כִּי אֵין כָּמֹהוּ בָּאָרֶץ
on earth,	
a blameless and upright man,	אִישׁ תָּם וְיָשָׁר
who fears God and shuns evil?"	יְרֵא אֱלֹהִים וְסָר מֵרָע

(2:3a)

This means that nothing has changed in Job's character and behavior.
He is now as he was then — word for word. Yet as He continues, God
reveals that much has indeed happened in the meanwhile. For He says:

64

"He still holds on to his integrity,
so you have incited Me against him
   to destroy him without cause."

וְעֹדֶנּוּ מַחֲזִיק בְּתֻמָּתוֹ
וַתְּסִיתֵנִי בוֹ לְבַלְּעוֹ חִנָּם

(2:3b)

In the expression חנם "without cause" God refers to the operative
words in Satan's claim "Does Job fear God חנם — for nought?" (1:9).
And as in Satan's question, so in God's reaction the word חנם denotes
both cause and effect. Satan asked: Does Job fear God without any
reason or purpose? And God answers: You incited Me against Job to
destroy him without reason or purpose.

In spite of God's resolute attitude, Satan is unconvinced. Not by
chance does he now come once again "to present himself before the
LORD"; he still has a claim:

Satan answered the LORD,
"Skin for skin — all that a man
   has he will give for his life."

וַיַּעַן הַשָּׂטָן אֶת־ה' וַיֹּאמַר
עוֹר בְּעַד־עוֹר וְכָל־אֲשֶׁר לָאִישׁ יִתֵּן
בְּעַד נַפְשׁוֹ

(2:4)

"Skin for skin" was probably a popular saying; parallels are known
from Arabic and Ugaritic. The phrase is best explained as originating in
the language of barter: the skin of one animal is exchanged for the skin of
another. According to this interpretation the saying fits in well with what
follows, that is, Satan's application of the saying to the situation: "All
that a man has he will give for his life", i.e., a man is willing to give all he
has, including his sons and his daughters, if his life is promised him in
return. It is typical, and psychologically understandable that, contrary to
the previous incident, Satan argues on the basis of "human" reason, using
a popular proverb. Now his charge is no longer a personal one against
Job, but a general one against mankind. Satan can no longer cast any
doubt on the unbroken faith that Job has demonstrated; he can no longer
cast aspersions on Job the individual, so he finds room for suspicion by
speaking of man in general, and having thus based his claim, he may
proceed from the general to the specific, to Job, and suggest:

"But put forth Your hand,
and touch his bone and his flesh
then will he not blaspheme You to
   Your face?"

אוּלָם שְׁלַח־נָא יָדְךָ
וְגַע אֶל־עַצְמוֹ וְאֶל־בְּשָׂרוֹ
אִם לֹא עַל פָּנֶיךָ יְבָרֲכֶךָּ

(2:5)

65

Once again, Satan suggests that the trial be through the personal action of God, And once again, God has no argument to counter Satan's assertion concerning mankind in general, nor to reject his application of it to Job in particular. He again agrees to Satan's suggestion, and again charges him with its execution:

The LORD said to Satan,
"See, he is in your power,"

וַיֹּאמֶר ה׳ אֶל־הַשָּׂטָן
הִנּוֹ בְיָדֶךָ

(2:6a)

That is, God again offers Satan more than Satan requested of God. Whereas Satan suggested "touch his bone and his flesh", God complies with "*he* is in your power", laying down but one condition:

"only spare his life."

אַךְ אֶת־נַפְשׁוֹ שְׁמֹר

(2:6b)

With that, the second heavenly scene comes to an end:

Satan left the presence of the LORD.

וַיֵּצֵא הַשָּׂטָן מֵאֵת פְּנֵי ה׳

(2:7a)

Scene V

(2:7b-13; 3:1)

We have already spoken of the difference between the transition from the first heavenly scene to the earthly scene that follows it, and the transition from the second earthly scene to the next earthly scene. We said that, in contrast to what preceded, there is no break in the narration between scenes IV and V. Immediately after "Satan left the presence of the LORD" (verse 7a), follows:

and smote Job with severe sores
from the sole of his foot to the crown
of his head.

וַיַּךְ אֶת־אִיּוֹב בִּשְׁחִין רָע
מִכַּף רַגְלוֹ וְעַד קָדְקֳדוֹ

(2:7b)

Thus the sentence with which the heavenly scene concludes is not an

66

independent sentence, but a clause contained in the compound sentence that constitutes verse 7. By explicitly marking the connection between the exit of Satan from the scene above and his smiting of Job with "severe sores", the narrator underscores the greatness of Job's spirit and his faith. In the first stage of the trial, Job is robbed of all he has, both by man and through the powers of nature. This is how the messengers view the disasters, but Job sees in them the hand of God. In his perception, all that was taken, "God has taken". And not only is he aware of this, he is also grateful, for he says, "Blessed be the name of the LORD". Thus Job's spiritual greatness and steadfastness are revealed at the conclusion of the first stage of his trial. In the second stage, the direct, unmediated link between the disaster and God is made clear. And though it is now impossible to attribute Job's plague to the evil of mankind or to the blind arbitrariness of nature — it can be attributed to God alone — Job's reaction remains the same as before.

The story wishes to emphasize the degree to which Job was aware of this direct connection as it is illustrated in the structure of verse 7. R. Yosef Kimchi interprets the verse "Satan left the presence of the LORD and smote Job with severe sores" as meaning "and the LORD smote Job", since the name of God, and not Satan, immediately precedes "and smote". Admittedly, the structure of the verse would permit R. Yosef Kimchi's interpretation, since biblical prose sometimes has compound sentences in which the object of the first clause serves as the subject of the second (compare, for example, II Kings 8:14). But in view of the subject matter, this interpretation is not appropriate to the verse. The disparity between the meaning of the verse and its literal reading is thus a result of a structural ambiguity, just as in the opening verse of the first stage of the trial (1:13). And, although less prominent, here, too, the ambiguity is intentional. The reader, who knows what Job does not, will understand what the sentence means, namely, that the subject of "smote" is the subject of the previous sentence: Satan. To Job, who does not know what the reader knows, the subject of the sentence is the object of the previous clause: the LORD. And yet, in spite of this, Job does not rise up against the LORD.

He took a potsherd to scrape himself,	וַיִּקַּח־לוֹ חֶרֶשׂ לְהִתְגָּרֵד בּוֹ
as he sat in the ashes. _(2:8)_	וְהוּא יֹשֵׁב בְּתוֹךְ־הָאֵפֶר

The second clause "as he sat in the ashes" is a subordinate clause describing a situation. The verse gives a tangible description of Job's external reaction, yet it is of no clear significance. It relates a very neutral detail while omitting the actual setting of the action. This method of mentioning "in passing" is characteristic of biblical narrative: only what is relevant to the understanding of the story is mentioned; details are omitted unless they have broader significance. By illustrating Job's physical, external reaction to his disease, the narrator points to the absence of any verbal reaction. The mention of Job sitting in the ashes enables the reader to empathize with Job's lot, to appreciate the anguish of his trial and to recognize Job's steadfastness. As has been pointed out, at the beginning of the first stage of the trial no mention is made of Job's whereabouts but rather those of his sons and daughters, with the implication that this is where Job is in spirit — a detail of deeper significance. Here, at the beginning of the second stage of the trial, it is Job's whereabouts that we are told of, for this is what is crucial to our understanding of the story.

When Job's spirit mourns, he suffers physical pain. Taking a potsherd to scrape himself, he sits among the ashes (as is customary, compare Jeremiah 6:26; Esther 4:3; Isaiah 58:5; Jonah 3:6), mourning his sons and daughters. And Job's pain is indeed great. Not only is he afflicted by great sorrow, but his disease is also extremely painful, whatever the exact nature of the severe שחין "sores", which is a subject of debate. To stress the unpleasantness of the disease, the verse does not call them simply "sores" but adds the adjective רע — vile, evil, severe (compare Deuteronomy 28:35). This type of affliction causes the sufferer to scrape the sores, and the scraping in turn causes greater pain. The second stage of the trial is more difficult than the first, for the afflictions are now greater than they were before. Spiritual anguish resulting directly from physical torment is greater than that which is an indirect result of material losses, even the loss of children. Furthermore, in the first stage of the trial (1:13), Job's whereabouts are given in an independent clause before the disasters are reported. In the second stage, his location is mentioned in a dependent clause (2:8b), while the main clause (2:8a) tells of his reaction to the latest blow. In the first trial, the calamities come crashing down like thunder on a clear day. The narrator prefaces the loss of wealth and family with an idyllic family tableau. In the second trial the disaster rubs salt into Job's wounds. The narrator portrays the mourner sitting in the ashes after describing in a subordinate clause, i.e. incidentally, his reaction to the disaster. The blow that descends from the blue leaves Job stunned, but he pulls himself out of his shock and is even able to bless God. However, the disaster that rubs salt into the wounds provokes rebellion. And yet Job does not rebel. He reveals no emotional reaction to the event. This time he is not comforted, neither does he bless God, but he does not blaspheme Him either. He suffers his intolerable pain in silence. Job is hushed. His silence is evidently a psychological defence against a rebellious outburst, preventing him from speaking out against God. As we have said, he is not only God-fearing but a human being as well. We may assume that, by now, Job's physical affliction and all the calamities that preceded it, must have aroused in him some doubt or misgivings. Yet he keeps silent, not permitting the thoughts in his soul to pass his lips.

Thus one must regard as a new trial the advice proferred to Job by his wife. Her speaking to him is in itself a trial, since in his emotional state Job can barely withold words and refrain from crying out. The trial is intensified because of what she says, and, further, because of who she is: his wife, the person closest to him, partner in joy and sorrow. It is she who addresses him:

His wife said to him,	וַתֹּאמֶר לוֹ אִשְׁתּוֹ
"You still hold on to your integrity?	עֹדְךָ מַחֲזִיק בְּתֻמָּתֶךָ
'Bless' God and die!"	בָּרֵךְ אֱלֹהִים וָמֻת

(2:9)

What does Job's wife mean to say? From the context it is clear that the meaning of ברך is not its literal sense "bless", nor does the imperative ומת "and die" mean what it appears to. The meaning of ברך is once again its opposite: blaspheme. The imperative form of the verb ומת "and die" is a result of the action expressed by the imperative form of the previous verb (compare Deuteronomy 32:49-50; Proverbs 3:3-4; etc.). What Job's wife means is: blaspheme God, for then you will die.

Different opinions have been expressed as to the character of Job's wife and her state of mind when she utters these words. Beginning with the Septuagint, where she is portrayed as giving a long speech, there have always been those who view her positively and those who criticize her. Augustine (Roman Church father, 354-430) compared Job's wife to Eve,

for like Eve she wished to incite her husband. He described her as
"*assistant* to Satan" (*diaboli adiutrix*). However, one cannot consider her
character or the emotional context of her words without exceeding the
bounds of scholarship. The narrator did not reveal his opinion of Job's
wife, for he had no interest in her — she is not even given a name —
although her torment was doubtless equal to Job's. As is customary with
the biblical storyteller, he relates only those details that can shed light on
the matter at hand. Of Job's wife we are told only what is necessary for
our proper understanding of how Job faced his trial. The commentator
cannot explain that which the author wished to leave unexplained. But the
narrator's choice of words, while it leaves a great deal unaccounted for,
does after all reveal a little. For the verse is structurally woven from sentence remnants of the deliberations that took place in heaven. His wife
says to him "You still hold on to your integrity"; God said of him "He
still holds on to his integrity" (2:3). His wife suggests " 'Bless' God";
Satan expresses his opinion of Job "He will 'bless' You to Your face"
(1:11; 2:5). By assigning to Job's wife two sentences whose origin are the
two opposing attitudes to Job in heaven, the narrator clarifies what appears inexplicable: her feelings, her suffering, her role in the drama. Thus
it appears that her suggestion to her husband is identical to what Satan
said about Job, but her motivation is different. Satan speaks out of pure
apostasy; Job's wife speaks out of pity. This is evident from the one
"original" word in her speech: the verb ומת "and die", which indicates the
purpose of her advice, different from that of Satan. Satan wishes to prove
that Job serves God only in order to receive reward. Job's wife wishes Job
to be relieved of his suffering. Her intention is good; her action is not. Job
— at least this time — does not understand his wife, and takes her words
not as she intends, but literally. Job's wife unwittingly becomes partner to
Satan.

However, this "emissary" of Satan also fails in her mission. Job's im-
mediate reaction to his wife's words is a reprimand:

He said to her,	וַיֹּאמֶר אֵלֶיהָ
"You speak as any of the shameless women might speak!	כְּדַבֵּר אַחַת הַנְּבָלוֹת תְּדַבֵּרִי
Shall we accept good from the hand of God and not accept evil?"	גַּם אֶת־הַטּוֹב נְקַבֵּל מֵאֵת הָאֱלֹהִים וְאֶת־הָרָע לֹא נְקַבֵּל

(2:10a)

In the first clause of his question גם את הטוב נקבל מאת האלהים the opening word גם — literally "also" — is problematic. Those who consider the
Masoretic version to be authentic assume that the word גם here, as
elsewhere when used at the beginning of biblical verses (Exodus 10:25;
Numbers 22:33; etc.), appears simply for emphasis, and that its meaning
can be rendered by the word "indeed!". In any case, the meaning of the
sentence is clear. It is a rhetorical question, just as the words of Job's wife
included a rhetorical question. Thus Job reacts to his wife's question with
one of his own. Her question was intended to shake his fear of God, his is
meant to strengthen it.

We are told how Job withstands this stage of his trial with the words:

For all this, Job did not sin   בְּכָל־זֹאת לֹא־חָטָא אִיּוֹב בִּשְׂפָתָיו
    with his lips.

(2:10b)

Raba explained this sentence thus (*Talmud Bab., Baba Batra* 16b):
"'With his lips' he did not sin, but in his heart he sinned". The same interpretation is reflected in the Targum. Scholars, however, consider this to
be a Midrashic interpretation, while according to the literal sense of the
verse, the words "with his lips" are not to be understood in the sense of
"as opposed to in his heart". This consensus of opinion is a result of two
basic assumptions that are characteristic of biblical criticism: the first is a
general rule of exegetical methodology; the second, in specific relation to
the book of Job, is a historical-literary consideration. According to the
first, a commonly accepted exegetical principle, style plays only an
aesthetic role, beautifying and embellishing the work, varying the modes
of expression in order to avoid monotony. The second, a widespread
literary-historical assumption in criticism of Job, is that the story in its
present form consists of two originally independent works: one, the prose
narrative that now forms the framework of the book, and the second, the
poetic body of the book. The two components of the book, it is main-
tained, were not adapted to each other with total consistency, hence the
evident contradiction in the description of Job's character. The Job of the
poetic component is a wise man who ponders, and even doubts, the
justice of God's ways in the world, while the Job of the narrative component is a perfect, righteous man whom no earthly tribulations can move
from his perfect and absolute faith in the justice of divine intervention.

One cannot, however, determine Job's character in the narrative according to the book's prehistory (even if the above is a reasonable theory and not mere conjecture), but according to proof found in the story as the final author wrote it. Such proof must be culled from the story in its totality, from content as well as style. Even if one rejects our theory of the role of style in literature in general, and in ancient or biblical literature in particular, and asserts that a word added or subtracted, similar or dissimilar, is a matter of embellishment or chance and therefore insignificant, even so, one cannot ignore the significance of the words "with his lips" in our verse. Since the use of stereotyped repetition is the *rule* in our story, so that sentences and verses are reiterated word for word, stylistic anomalies must have significance and cannot be merely a technique to avoid monotony. Therefore, in order to understand Job's reaction to the second stage of the trial, in order to appraise his character and the strength of his faith after his wife speaks to him, one must take seriously the narrator's comment in his closing sentence, and consider the words "with his lips".

It is particularly unsound method to ignore these words in view of the fact that they do not occur in the previous, corresponding comment (1:22). Nor is this the only difference between the two verses. Compare:

(1:22) For all this Job did not sin, nor did he cast reproach upon God.
(2:10) For all this, Job did not sin with his lips.

The two are both similar and different. Each one lacks something and adds something. The first lacks "with his lips" and adds "nor did he cast reproach upon God"; the second — vice versa. In each one what is added is expressed in what is missing; as a result of what is missing we infer the addition. This intentional difference in the style of the narrator's comment makes no sense unless we assume that he was precise in his phrasing and added or subtracted not merely to vary his style but in order to illustrate through the style that a change had indeed taken place in Job, that is, "with his lips" he did not sin, but in his heart he did. The narrator understood that the emotional stability which Job demonstrated after the first stage of his trial was a psychological impossibility after the second, that Job cannot be as stable after what he has discovered as he was when he still possessed everything. After Satan's actions, and after his wife's words, Job may not sin "with his lips". But in his heart — over which

72

even Job has no control — he will sin, will raise questions about God's ways.

And indeed, this point, expressed by what is contained in the narrator's closing comment as well as by what goes unsaid, is contained also in the story of the second stage of the trial itself. In her rhetorical question (verse 9a), Job's wife, as we said, wishes to shake her husband's faith, and Job, in his question to her (verse 10b), wishes to reinforce not only her faith but also — perhaps primarily — his own. Psychological observation would suggest that the rational claim which Job presents in order to reject his wife's suggestion is actually directed toward dispelling those thoughts that are in his own mind. This suggestion is not only the logical result of psychological considerations, it is, more importantly, implied in Job's own words. If we compare what Job says in 2:10 "Shall we accept good from the hand of God and not accept evil?" with his words at the end of the first stage of the trial (1:21) "Naked came I out of my mother's womb and naked shall I return there; the LORD gave, the LORD has taken away; blessed be the name of the LORD", we shall see that in both cases Job's claim is a rational one, an attempt to force his mind to influence his feelings. But whereas in the first case he speaks three sentences, here he speaks but one. His words in the first instance are personal and tangible; here, they are general and abstract. In the first sentence the subject is I, Job; in the second, and actually in the third as well, it is God; here, the subject is We, man in general, and God is only the indirect object. Here Job speaks of "good" and "evil" that we must accept; previously, neither good nor evil was mentioned but rather God's giving and taking away. Job's earlier utterance was a reaction not to the words of those around him but to the action — or inaction — of the All-Present God. Here, they are a reaction to the words of someone present. The previous claim was phrased in declarative sentences followed by an exclamation, a declaration; here, the claim is a negative question, eliciting a negative answer, probably interrogative, but perhaps declarative. The earlier phrasing revealed through its grammar and otherwise that Job's emotional equilibrium had indeed been shaken but that he had slowly regained it and had arrived at the necessary conclusion: "Blessed be the name of the LORD". Here, no conclusion is reached, a clear sign of the deterioration in his emotional equilibrium. The differing reactions to disaster reflect fluctuation in the soul of Job, a wavering of faith which began when his happiness began to fade. Nonetheless, he has not yet blasphemed God "to His face"; he has not sinned with his lips. The commonly held view that the Job of our story is a man whose righteousness remains static from beginning to end, is not consistent with the story itself. Although the didactic aim of the story might require the existence and collapse of a philosophy that is based on imagination and speculation to be concretized in purely legendary figures and motifs, nonetheless, in order to make the conclusion not merely theoretical but also, and primarily, of practical value in life, the characterization of the protagonist and his reaction to the world must be built upon real human nature.

All that Job has suffered so far signifies a reversal of Wisdom's rationalistic and utilitarian philosophy of reward and punishment: evil has struck him despite his righteousness. The new reality created by the works of Satan has called into question Wisdom's perception of divine rule. But Job gives a new interpretation of existence, based on what has occurred, and thus regains his self-control. Will he continue to hold fast to his opinion even if called upon to defend and prove it? He easily dismisses his wife's words: his rebuke silences her immediately. Will he hold fast to his new outlook when the champions of Wisdom's doctrine of recompense appear?

The arrival of Job's friends, with which the story closes (verses 11-13), is an integral part of this organic prologue to the book. Admittedly, the story itself contains no mention of the ensuing dispute, but its basis has been laid and it has been anticipated psychologically. While the trial that has just ended in Job dismissing the words of the challenger (his wife) came as a result of his wife's utterance, the next trial, destined to continue in disputation, comes into being as a consequence of the *silence* of the challenger (the friends). It was Job's wife, the person closest to him, who brought about the trial that ended in her being silenced, i.e., overcome; the friends, who came from afar, are to bring about a trial that will develop into a prolonged struggle:

When Job's three friends heard about these calamities that had befallen him,	וַיִּשְׁמְעוּ שְׁלֹשֶׁת רֵעֵי אִיּוֹב אֵת כָּל־הָרָעָה הַזֹּאת הַבָּאָה עָלָיו
each came from his home — Eliphaz the Temanite, Bildad	וַיָּבֹאוּ אִישׁ מִמְּקֹמוֹ אֱלִיפַז הַתֵּימָנִי וּבִלְדַּד

the Shuhite, and Zophar the Naamathite.   הַשּׁוּחִי וְצוֹפַר הַנַּעֲמָתִי
They met together to come to mourn   וַיִּוָּעֲדוּ יַחְדָּו לָבוֹא לָנוּד־לוֹ וּלְנַחֲמוֹ
with him and to comfort him.

(2:11)

Eliphaz comes from Teman, from the south; Bildad from Shuah, apparently in the east (see Genesis 25:2); and Zophar from Naamah, which is presumably in the north. Like the four messengers, the three friends come from different directions. But whereas the messengers came in succession, the friends arrive at the same time, for we read "they met together". The messengers came to report to Job the loss of his property and children; the friends come לנוד לו ולנחמו "to mourn with him and to comfort him". Both verbs, which form an alliteration, appear together later in the book (42:11). The verb נוד assumed its connotation of "to express sympathy with the troubles of one's fellow" (Isaiah 51:19; Jeremiah 15:5; 48:17; Nahum 3:7; Psalm 69:21) from the widespread practice of expressing feelings of grief, either spontaneously or as a convention, by nodding one's head. Expressing sympathy and consolation are not only a natural manifestation of friendship, they are also an observance prescribed by society. When Job appears to his friends, they do not know him. His agony has so distorted his appearance that even from afar it is noticeable:

When they looked up from a distance,   וַיִּשְׂאוּ אֶת־עֵינֵיהֶם מֵרָחוֹק
they did not recognize him;   וְלֹא הִכִּירֻהוּ
they wept aloud.   וַיִּשְׂאוּ קוֹלָם וַיִּבְכּוּ

(2:12a)

Then, after the natural, personal reaction, comes the conventional response when one is confronted with misfortune:

Each one tore his coat,   וַיִּקְרְעוּ אִישׁ מְעִלוֹ
and they threw dust over their heads   וַיִּזְרְקוּ עָפָר עַל רָאשֵׁיהֶם הַשָּׁמָיְמָה
toward the sky.

(2:12b)

Placing dust on one's head at a time of tragedy was a widespread custom in biblical times, not only in Israel (see Joshua 7:6; Ezekiel 27:30; Lamentations 2:10). Our verse differs, however, from other references to the same custom in two details: (a) The verb by which the action is denoted is different. The customary verb is העלה "put up"; here, the verb

75

used is זרק, Job's friends "throw" dust on their heads; (b) The dust is used differently: in other contexts a mourner puts the dust *on* his head; here we are told that the characters throw dust *over* their heads toward the sky. Biblical critics agree that the word השמימה "toward the sky" is an addition in the Masoretic text (in the Septuagint it does not appear), arguing that the severe sores with which Job was afflicted reminded some later reader of the plague of "boils" (שחין) in Egypt, where, we are told, Moses threw the soot from the furnace heavenwards: "The Lᴏʀᴅ said to Moses and Aaron, 'Each of you take handfuls of soot from the furnace and let Moses throw it *toward the sky* השמימה in the sight of Pharoah. It shall become fine dust throughout the land of Egypt, and ... shall become boils שחין ...'" (Exodus 9:8). Influenced by the verse in Exodus, the "later" reader recorded alongside our verse the marginal comment השמימה — "toward the sky" — which eventually made its way from the margin into the text through a copyist's negligence, or else a punctilious copyist may have written it at the end of the verse to indicate that it was an interpolation. According to this commonly accepted opinion, the original text said that Job's friends all tore their coats and threw dust upon their heads, following the general custom. But this explanation for the addition השמימה does not account for the use of the verb "throw". Perhaps we should assume that throwing dust over their heads toward the sky was not an expression of mourning at all, but rather, just as in the case of Moses, the imitation of a prevalent type of magic, "sympathetic magic". This magic is based on the theory that one action induces another similar one. The result of throwing soot from the furnace heavenwards was that it fell back to earth not as soot, but as something similar — boils. (In the case of the plague of boils, Moses' action is not really magic but merely symbolic, for the boils do not appear automatically, as a result of the magical power of throwing the soot into the sky, but rather as a result of the sovereign will of God: the symbolic act, however, is clearly an imitation of the magical act.) In addition, such magic serves not only to induce something similar, but also to remove something similar. Thus it is possible that the action of Job's friends, described in the words "threw dust into the sky over their heads", is a magical act of self-defense: in order to ensure that the sores with which Job is afflicted "from the sole of his foot to the crown of his head" will not fall from heaven on them as well, they throw dust over their heads into the sky as they approach Job.

As the friends arrive at Job's side,

They sat down with him on the ground for seven days and seven nights,	וַיֵּשְׁבוּ אִתּוֹ לָאָרֶץ שִׁבְעַת יָמִים וְשִׁבְעָה לֵילוֹת
and none spoke a word to him,	וְאֵין דֹּבֵר אֵלָיו דָּבָר
for they saw that his suffering was very great.	כִּי רָאוּ כִּי־גָדַל הַכְּאֵב מְאֹד

(2:13)

In order to explain their behavior, modern commentators compare the Arab custom in caring for the sick: "If the illness continues for a long time during the dry season, the relatives bring the ill one to a high heap of garbage on the outskirts of the village, and they build a thatched awning above him ... there the patient lies, sometimes for days and nights on end ... when the news of his illness spreads friends and relatives come immediately to visit him and form a circle around him. There is silence; no one speaks; they only listen to his sighs and complaints. Only when he turns and speaks to them do they reply, mourning his situation. But even then not all of them; only the aged among them. The others almost do not dare to join in the discussion".[14] From this description one might conclude, as do most commentators, that the silence of Job's friends is merely an accepted custom observed when visiting the sick. The friends' behavior serves as the precedent for the Rabbinic law: "Those who come to comfort are not permitted to speak until the mourner speaks first, as is said, 'and after this Job opened his mouth'" (*Talmud Bab., Moed Ųatan* 28b). Job's friends, however, were unaware not only of this Talmudic law but of the Arabic custom as well; this is clear from the explanation given for their silence: "for they saw that his suffering was very great". The friends' silence is none other than sincere sympathy for the sorrow and trouble of their comrade, complete identification with his situation. In the same manner, "the elders of the daughters of Zion" sit in silence (Lamentations 2:10), since the pain of the destruction shocks them to the point that they are unable even to weep. When Job's friends look up from afar, they raise their voices and weep; but when they sit with Job they weep no more, nor do they try to comfort him. Though their purpose in coming is "to mourn with him and to comfort him" (verse 11), in the end "none spoke a word

14. A. Musil, *Arabia Petraea*, III, Vienna 1908, p. 413.

to him, for they saw that his suffering was very great". To consider the silence of Job's friends as simply a social convention observed when visiting the sick or the mourner, would be to ignore what the verse says and to disregard the dialectic and dynamics of the story. Such a view would prevent the reader from perceiving the tragic irony in Job's misunderstanding of his friends' behavior, and without this perception, neither the role of this irony nor of the last scene as a whole can be grasped, and the storyteller's artistic skill and psychological insight go unappreciated. For from the terrible silence of seven days and seven nights that weighed upon the spirits of the mourners, it was inevitable that bitterness, resentment, and even rebellion should accumulate within Job's heart, so that when his distress reaches its pinnacle — and this is what is meant by the period of "seven days and seven nights" — it is impossible for him to hold back his outburst any longer. Forced by unbearable pressure, Job must open his mouth, and what he utters is a curse:

After this Job opened his mouth,	אַחֲרֵי־כֵן פָּתַח אִיּוֹב אֶת־פִּיהוּ
and cursed his day.	וַיְקַלֵּל אֶת־יוֹמוֹ

(3:1)

Just as the words אחרי כן "after this" in the verse "and after this his brothers talked with him" (Genesis 45:15) open the sentence which tells how Joseph's brothers broke their shocked silence, so does the expression אחרי כן here open the sentence in which Job relieves the tension that has become intolerable. Bowed under the weight of an oppressive silence, and under the pressure of the thoughts that must by now have cried out in his mind, "Job opened his mouth". The expression "opened his mouth", like the expression "opened his lips" (Job 11:5; 32:21), is a poetic idiom for the action expressed in prose by the verb "to speak". But, while the expression "opened his lips" only illustrates what is expressed in the verb "to speak", the expression "opened his mouth" can also indicate an active decision to break a silence. This is apparently indicated by the fact that only the expression "opened his mouth", and never "opened his lips", is used to convey the opposite of keeping silent (Isaiah 53:7; Psalm 38:14; 39:10; cf. Job 33:2). Thus, Job's decision to break the silence is implicit in "Job opened his mouth"; the same is suggested by the context: "*After this* Job opened his mouth" follows "and none spoke a word to him, for they saw that his suffering was very great".

78

The last direct information we had of Job followed his reaction to his wife's words: "For all this, Job did not sin with his lips" (2:10); he did not curse God to His face. When, in reaction to the silence of his friends, he does open his mouth, is it possible that he will not sin with his lips? Thus far he has not cursed God, now he curses — but only "his day", his existence itself (compare Job 30:55), the existence to which he has been sentenced, but not the Judge who issued the decree.

Some commentators see in the expression "After this" a seam with which the author joins the prologue story with the poetic debate that forms the main section of the book, since the same expression is used occasionally in the Bible as an editorial device to connect originally independent narratives. If however, this transitional verse is indeed a seam connecting the story with the ensuing dispute, the author has used a common editorial technique as a personal touch to the text, to lend emphasis.

CONCLUSION

Scholarship concerned with the book of Job is agreed, we have noted, that the story which appears here is adapted from another which antedates the main body of the book, the debate. Our analysis of the story has repeatedly demonstrated that if the story is an adaptation, it is a highly artistic one, carefully thought out and executed by a master hand. It is possible that the story written by the author of the book of Job did not *originate* with him, that it stems from earlier sources, but his treatment of it is beyond doubt *original*, since the story that the author supposedly drew upon served as raw material only, which he moulded to his intentions and stamped with his image. The author's genius is no less evident in the way in which he links his adapted story with his original work, i.e., in the use of the story as a prologue to the book, as the opening of the debate. For the conclusion of the story, the silence of the friends which induces Job to "curse his day", opens the debate that forms the last stage of the trial which Job must withstand before his reaction to God's ways brings God's answer to man's questioning of world order, which is the central problem in the book. Indeed, the author has made a unified work of the three sections of the book, the prologue, the body, and the epilogue, whatever their origin may have been. The unity can be seen not only in the content, in the consistency of thought and spirit, but also in the structure, with its skillful transitions.

We recall that at the beginning of the story Job was represented as possessing four characteristics, corresponding to the four pairs of blessings which he enjoyed. In the first stage of the trial four messengers come and report the four disasters through which the four blessings were lost. Corresponding to the four messengers announcing Satan's fourfold deed, four partners to Satan appear in the second stage of the trial: Job's wife and his three friends. But unlike the four catastrophes of the first stage, only three visitations constitute the second: the sores, the wife's words, and the friends' silence — yet according to the structure of the story one would expect one more factor in the trial. But Job's trial does not end with the silence of his friends; it continues and reaches its climax in their speech, in their attack, but of this the story makes no mention. The story prepares us for it, for it is the subject of the body of the book. Thus the accusations and defense which made up the poetic section are psychologically tied to the opening story.

To reinforce the literary continuity, the author uses a stylistic device found frequently in the Bible, the "guide-word" (*Leitwort*). The two guide-words found in the story are (a) the verb ברך and (b) the adverb חנם. The verb ברך appears in the story six times: 1:5 (= blaspheme); 1:10 (= bless); 1:11 (= blaspheme); 1:21 (= bless); 2:5 (= blaspheme); 2:9 (= blaspheme). By using the root ברך six times in its two antithetical meanings, the author makes clear what he considers the subject of the story to be: the investigation of two questions which are in effect one. The first, which is more explicit, relates to man's blessing God; the second, only implied, relates to God's blessing man. The first question asks: Is man's blessing God — whether "bless" is meant literally or not — dependent upon God's blessing man? And the question which is only implied: Is God's blessing man dependent upon man's blessing Him? In "the Land of Uz", where instances of both God's blessing of man and man's blessing of God are in abundance, the questions are not asked. This is why the issue is raised in heaven and why the events on earth take place, so that the second question can be raised on earth, and, in response to it, the first also can be answered. Although in the story itself no one asks the second question, Job, in his first reaction, answers it: "Blessed be the name of the LORD".

As for the reason why the verb ברך appears just six times — and not seven, which is the perfect number — it would seem that, since the story is not only an independent unit, but also the prologue of a larger work, the book of Job, the six instances of ברך in the prologue are complemented by the seventh and final mention, in the epilogue: "The LORD ברך blessed the latter end of Job more than his beginning" (42:12).

While the first guide-word is used as a device to connect the prologue and the epilogue, the second guide-word does the same for the story and the debate which follows. In the story, the adverb חנם is used twice in heaven. Satan uses it in the first dialogue: "Does Job fear God *for nought?*" (1:9). God uses it in the second: "You have incited me against him to destroy him *without cause*" (2:3). Both use the term חנם in its double meaning: without reason, and for no purpose. When the events on earth are related, the term חנם is not used, but appears in the debate; here, too, it appears twice and in the words of two opponents. Eliphaz, who sees in Job's situation the revelation of God's justice, and the punishment for Job's sin, says to Job "For you have taken pledges from your brother חנם" — without reason, and without basis (22:6). Job, however, who sees in his fate the revelation of God's supremacy, manifested in his suffering without having sinned, says of God "He multiplies my wounds חנם" — for nought, without reason, without basis (9:17).

There is thus a debate in heaven: does true fear of God for its own sake exist or not? In order to resolve this heavenly debate, Satan, on God's authority, destroys the logical, harmonious, ethical world of "the Land of Uz", which, being a speculative construction, the creation of the "wise" over-sophisticated man in his own image, has no basis in reality. This imaginary world is destroyed, but only for Job. His friends continue to believe that it exists, as real as ever.

On earth the debate still rages: is there an ethical basis to God's behavior or not? Is the doctrine of "Wisdom" true or not? Eliphaz believes that God's behavior is based on justice, and that Job's situation proves this since he had taken pledges from his brother חנם "for nought". But Job no longer sees in this world of "Wisdom" anything more than an illusion. Even so, all that has taken place before his eyes is no more than the blind and deaf chaos of God's arbitrary dealing: Job's situation proves this, for God "multiplies his wounds חנם — without cause". Yet he refuses to accept what he sees, and he cannot accept what his friends say. He therefore searches and beseeches God, demanding to be shown the whole truth, the world's eternal truth. In order to settle the controversy on earth, God will appear to Job and will show him the world in all its stark reality. On the surface it is illogical, disharmonious, unethical. Yet the heart will comprehend that all the details of the world complement each other, forming one unified whole, each and every detail "good" in itself, and in its entirety "very good", complete, perfect, and, as a creation of God, as incomprehensible as its Creator.

82

BIBLIOGRAPHY

In addition to the commentaries of Rashi and Ibn Ezra, found in all editions of *Miqraot Gedolot*, mention should be made of the commentaries published by I. Schwarz in תקות אנוש, Berlin 1862.

I would suggest the following modern commentaries:

Hebrew: א' כהנא, ספר איוב, תל־אביב תרפ"ח; מ"צ סגל, איוב, תל־אביב תש"א; עמוס חכם, ספר איוב, ירושלים תש"ל.

English: M. H. Pope, *Job* (*The Anchor Bible*, 15), New York 1965; E. Dhorme, *Job*, Leiden 1967.

French: E. P. Dhorme, *Le Livre de Job* (*Études Bibliques*), Paris 1926.

German: A. Weiser, *Das Buch Hiob* (*Das Alte Testament Deutsch*, 13)[3], Göttingen 1959; G. Fohrer, *Das Buch Hiob* (*Kommentar zum Alten Testament*, 16), Gütersloh 1963; F. Horst, *Hiob*, [Chapters I-XIX] (*Biblischer Kommentar — Altes Testament*, XVI/1), Neukirchen-Vluyn 1968.

Mention should be made of the following literature:

Hebrew: י' קויפמן, תולדות האמונה הישראלית, כרך שני/ספר שני, תל־אביב תש"ו, עמ' 604 ואילך; מ' בובר, תורת הנביאים[2], תל־אביב תש"י, עמ' 172 ואילך; מ' בובר, דרכו של מקרא, ירושלים תשכ"ד, עמ' 340 ואילך.

English: Y. Kaufmann, *The Religion of Israel* (translated and abridged by M. Greenberg), Chicago 1960, pp. 334-338; M. Buber, *The Prophetic Faith*, New York 1949, pp. 188-197; W. Eichrodt, *Theology of the Old Testament*, I, London 1961, II, London 1967 (see index); G. von Rad, *Old Testament Theology*, I, Edinburgh 1963, pp. 408-418; idem, *Wisdom in Israel*, London 1972, pp. 206-226; 237-239.

German: M. Buber, *Der Glaube der Propheten*, Zürich 1950, pp. 170-282 (= *Werke*, II, München 1957, pp. 405-415); W. Eichrodt, *Theologie des Alten Testaments*, I⁵, Göttingen 1957, II-III⁴, Göttingen 1961 (see index); G. von Rad, *Theologie des Alten Testaments*, I, München 1957, pp. 405-415; idem, *Weisheit in Israel*, Neukirchen-Vluyn 1970, pp. 267-292; 306-308.

For the principles of the method of "Total Interpretation" see: מ' וייס, המקרא כדמותו, ירושלים תשכ"ז; M. Weiss, "Die Methode der 'Total-Interpretation'", *Supplements to Vetus Testamentum*, XVII (1972), pp. 88-122; idem, *The Bible from Within — The Method of Total Interpretation*, Jerusalem (in print).